PAIN

JOURNEYS AROUND MY PARENTS

November 4, 2000

To Bill —

written in smiles and tears

Keith

PAIN

JOURNEYS AROUND MY PARENTS

Keith Garebian

mosaic press

Canadian Cataloguing in Publication Data

Garebian, Keith, 1943-
Pain: journeys around my parents

ISBN 0-88962-709-6

1. Garebian, Keith, 1943- . 2. Bombay (India) - Social life and customs. 3. Theater critics - Canada - Biography. 4. Authors, Canadian (English) - 20th century - Biography .*
I. Title.

PN1708.G37A32000 792'.092 C00-931958-1

Published by Mosaic Press, offices and warehouse at 1252 Speers Road, Units 1 and 2, Oakville, Ontario, L6L 5N9, Canada and Mosaic Press, PMB 145, 4500 Witmer Industrial Estates, Niagara Falls, NY, 14305-1386, U.S.A.

Mosaic Press acknowledges the assistance of the Canada Council and the Department of Canadian Heritage, Government of Canada for their support of our publishing programme.

Printed and Bound in Canada

MOSAIC PRESS CANADA:
1252 Speers Road, Units 1 & 2,
Oakville, Ontario, L6L 5N9
Canada
Ph/Fax: 905-825-2130
editorial:
cp507@freenet.toronto.on.ca
orders & service:
mosaicpress@on.aibn.com

MOSAIC PRESS U.S.A.:
PMB 145
4500 Witmer Industrial Estates
Niagara Falls, NY, 14305-1386
U.S.A.
Ph/Fax: 1-800-387-8992
editorial:
cp507@freenet.toronto.on.ca
orders & service:
mosaicpress@on.aibn.com

Le Conseil des Arts du Canada | The Canada Council for the Arts

For my son, Michael

where is the angel
with the news that the river
is coming back,
the angel with the word
that the water will be clear
and have fish

– Peter Balakian

ACKNOWLEDGMENTS

Raw material came from many sources, some of which are clearly indicated in the text. However, I would especially like to thank the following writers for permission to quote from their works: Lorne Shirinian, whose *History of Armenia and Other Fictions* proved to be a rewarding read, and Perseus Books for passages from Peter Balakian's *Black Dog of Fate*.

Colleagues and friends read the manuscript in earlier versions and offered helpful advice, so I add their names in gratitude: John Metcalf, Kenneth Sherman, Jack David, and Henry Beissel. I have no one to blame but myself for any literary foibles or defects that remain in the work.

A special token of gratitude goes to my publisher, Howard Aster, who has continued to show faith in my work and who has published what is guaranteed to have only a very small readership but one, I hope, that values writers who take risks.

AUTHOR'S NOTE

This is a memoir whose tone is intimate, its non-linear narrative broken at times into poetry and meditation. It has a bifurcated external structure—the first section being set in India, the second in Armenia. While I was, in a radical sense, not truly at home in the first (my birthplace), I was even more distanced from the second, not having set foot on any Armenian soil and not knowing any Armenian history (apart from my father's eye-witness accounts of genocide). Therefore, it would be accurate to say that the settings are primarily mental, conjured up from fragmented personal memories, eyewitness reports, and strangers' texts, steeped in emotion, and not ever purporting to be the whole truth (which is itself a mythical concept).

We are prone to forget our beginnings, especially those which carry bad news of the world. This memoir attempts to retrieve certain traces of my beginnings, and so it should be read as a journey of self-discovery, even though it is about my parents.

There is a common view that memoirs should be written exclusively by celebrities or significant public figures—as if their lives were somehow more than beads on the never-ending string of time. But we are all significant because we live in an age of significant tremors—not simply earthquakes in India, Iran, or Turkey, but cosmos-shaking upheavals around the globe: holocausts, world wars, assassinations, and routine cruelties. And some of us have survived—just barely—mankind's great strides towards self-obliteration.

There are other no less significant tremors: those of cultural, geographical, and psychic dispossession, those of alienation from foe and beloved, stranger and kin.

In such an age it is easy to lose faith, for even the Kabbala reports that this is a shattered universe, one of splintered and scattered vessels. God is hidden, if not exiled; and evil, rather than good, continues to be perceived clearly.

This book is my attempt to keep faith with my parents and their joys and pains. It is also an attempt to keep faith with the written word, for memory not transfigured by language is dim light peeping feebly through the pores of broken vessels that are buried under centuries of cosmic dust. In the internal fugual structure of this memoir there is an implicit conviction that writing is a redemption of exile, estrangement, grief, anger, loss, and death. The design is not quite as casual as it may appear to be, and the epigraphs serve as clues as to that overall design. As an extended meditation in various modes, it is a literary memoir because it is an attempt to discover a form out of moments of memory.

This is a son's memoir, but it is also about that son's writing of one.

– KEITH GAREBIAN
MISSISSAUGA, 2000

"...the 'writerly' or experimental text cannot be read any one way and does not have controlled and controllable meaning."

– Stanley Fogel

"Words do not simply and directly interpret the world (even if there were an interpretable world). There is no recourse to originary meaning or originary presence in order to prove something or discover a truth."

– Stanley Fogel

"(W)rite of consciousness."

– b.p. Nichol

"The child you have been will never desert you."

– Andrew O'Hagan

"Ambiguity. Redundance. Irrelevance, even. Leakage."

– Thomas Pynchon

"We make out of the quarrel with others, rhetoric; but out of the quarrel with ourselves, poetry."

– W.B. Yeats

"Just the worst time of the year/For a journey, and such a long journey."

– T.S. Eliot

"Against despair."

– Samuel Johnson's final journal

PART ONE

January 1991

Fresh snow one night in January, and my mother died. I wept, and I have not done with weeping.

We found her in the dead of winter, dying without naming eternity. Then, when no birdsong fluted its way from any snow-worn twig, when no azure leaked from veins of sky, she became the source of this creation, arranging by her dying the subjects I could twine into hard particulars of passion, the stubborn facts of my memorial being.

This once she is bound to my meaning, ephemera sliding into my ephemera. Grief moved my words into place, recalling time in little flames.

Her physician told us there was no hope. The pneumonia could not be fought off in her emphysemic condition. Moreover, she did not want to be kept alive by a machine.

Her room had the typical clean white look and smell of an astringent chamber, yet there seemed to be too much tidiness for her death. There were charts and tubes, soundless machines and needles. She looked like a feeble puppet on strings, as her small hands tried to trace their own semaphore, attempting to push away the plastic tubes from her frail skin.

As she moaned, groaned, gasped for air, her eyes remained closed. Carbon dioxide was building in her lungs, billowing through her respiratory system.

The sounds she made were a grotesque attempt to expel the carbon dioxide.

I had never heard my mother groan like this before. Only once had I ever heard her moan. That was almost ten years earlier, when my sister, Elma, the middle one of her three children, had succumbed to cancer.

My parents, their age multiplied by grief, had wept at her coffin. Their bodies had heaved and sagged.

After that, my mother aged a decade in a single year. The soft beauty in her small, round face gave way to seams of pain.

My brother-in-law, Peter, had phoned earlier in the evening after I had just returned from an interview with an actor in Niagara-on-the-Lake. She was going to stay in hospital, he said without any sense of alarm; it was simply precautionary to monitor her breathing because she had a touch of pneumonia. "Well, then, I'll see her tomorrow," I promised.

Her energy had begun to run down, I knew full well, and of late there was always the expectation that she would need a respirator if her emphysema clogged her lungs. Tiny and frail, she had a cloud of grey hair around her head, and as she was growing increasingly fatigued, though never without humour.

She had lived with my sister, Audrey, and her husband, quite content with her small room on the ground floor, directly opposite the door leading to the carpetted basement where the fireplace, sofa, and couch made for a snug haven in which she could watch television game shows, particularly *Let's Make a Deal* with Monty Hall and *The Price is Right* with silvering Bob Barker. All her belongings could fit into a makeshift closet, an emblem of her reduced world. She didn't have much: a few family photographs, chiefly of her childhood and ours–my sister's and mine–inexpensive knick-knacks, cheap jewellery, her inexpensive coats and dresses, woollen cardigans, and old shoes. Because of her small feet, the shoes had had to be bought in Youth Footwear departments. They, like the dresses and jewellery, had been retained against long odds. For my mother, they were fragments of a lifetime in which too much had been carelessly jettisoned.

She had gone to live with my youngest sister after a heroic decision to separate from my father, a man who hoarded junk as tenaciously as he shored up violent resentments and paranoid suspicions. She had simply packed up her most valued possessions in little boxes and left him to his animosities. Walked out after forty-five years of a marriage that must have been an unbearable onslaught against her mild forbearance. Despite her winsomeness, she could be determined when she needed to be.

Though she received letters and cards from friends abroad, she never sent them any, hoping that they would eventually give up on her and stop sending her mail. She didn't feel that she should explain to anyone her personal reasons for her breaking away from my father. She was never–could not ever be–an Armenian wife. To begin with, she was *odar*, an outsider by virtue of ethnic background, language, and culture. She was not what his people called *jarbig*; wit she had, but not the energy or vitality to match his. And she was not quite *achgapatz*, open-eyed in the sense that she could be fiercely protective at the gate to the home. The family was precious to her, yes, but she was never a fighter.

Thirteen years younger than him, she couldn't take any more of his nagging about her chronic smoking. He smoked too, sometimes cadging cigarettes from her, often forgetting that the ash from his cigarette was two inches long, but he believed that his habit had a proportionality lacking in hers. Moreover, she was the emphysemic one, lacking his robust appetites and unwilling to accompany him on his daily excursions to the local mall.

"I still cannot figure out why she married Adam," my aunt Pat wondered in a recent letter to me from England.

She was easy to satisfy, particularly with the companionship of her two grandchildren, whereas my father had too many sullen moods and could often be sunk in a sour reverie in the midst of a family conversation. She never waxed philosophical, preferring to live her simple life according to her private wisdom, whereas he was full of tirades against real or imagined antagonists: the "lazy" superintendent, the "swines" of corporate management, the "dirty" neighbours who didn't push their garbage down the incinerator chute, the "funny" friends who had not been quick enough to refill his glass at the last family dinner. "Funny" was his code word for distasteful or insulting behaviour.

"I'm leaving."

Had she actually phrased it so plainly, so daringly? She had, in her own small way, changed worlds, making another beginning late in life.

He had thought that he had won, for while she would have to eat the crust of humility with her daughter and son-in-law, he would enjoy total possession of the three-bedroom apartment that she had set up. Her existence would surely be regulated by the regimen of others, whereas he revelled in the secret hope that he would punish her by forcing her to change her life.

"He thinks I'll soon be bored or frustrated and go back to him," she used to remark with quiet humour. She knew that he counted on the fact that her pitiably small pension would not sustain her needs, but he overlooked the fact of her modest needs. Most of all, she wanted peace and harmony, things that he could not offer consistently. Besides, money was not her preoccupation, though it was certainly his, for the Armenian way to have money is to save every cent you make. "His attitude to money was interesting," comments my brother-in-law, Peter. "He would go to great pains to save money, but when he felt generous, he would spend it." He would sometimes give his two grandchildren gifts of $1,000, yet it was nothing for him to make a dozen trips a day to stores which would save him 40¢ on a carton of cigarettes."

My mother could not reconcile herself to this paradox. She had also learned what my father should have known in his bones: don't get too attached to places in life.

She knew there would be no going back. The psychic break was decisive.

The comic irony was that my sister's house on Brentwood Drive in Brampton was a two-minute drive from the apartment on Lisa Road; yet, the few hundred yards were a continental divide for my mother.

Eventually, of course, my father realized that he needed her more than he would ever admit.

"When are you coming back?" he asked, attempting to control the humiliation he felt for having to beg. At first, the question sounded like a mild inquiry, a casual curiosity. It was as if she were just away on a visit and needed to get back. But then this changed to an acknowledgement that he was punished, though he tended to regard her conduct as a theatrical display of independence and protest which should be ended. When it finally dawned on him that there would be no reunion, he experienced spasms of bitter vindictiveness, refusing to allow my sister or her husband to collect a few more of my mother's belongings from the apartment. Whenever Audrey or Peter made their weekly visits, he would complain that something or other was missing. "Did you take anything the last time you were here?" Loneliness exacerbated his malevolent suspiciousness.

These memories flooded into me when I sped to the hospital after Peter's second phone-call had come a mere half hour after the first.

"I've got bad news, I'm afraid," he had begun, but even before his words fell like a weight across my heart, I sensed from his almost hushed pitch that he was struggling against horror. "She's not going to make it."

I was terrified I would arrive too late, and in my haste, with tears splashing down my cheeks, as the snow began to fall in soft feathers, I didn't think of my father.

I rushed to Emergency, but it was the wrong entrance. Despair welled within me, as I finally parked my car and ran to the front desk where the placid receptionist directed me to the correct floor and wing.

My teenage son and his mother had beaten me there, but they had not been allowed to enter the room. My sister soon joined us with my mother's physician, and I was given a quick medical summary.

"Can't you give her a needle?" I asked, surprised by my own anguished vehemence.

The doctor misheard me or misunderstood. She went on about the need to respect my mother's wishes. But I had meant a tranquillizing agent, something, anything to allay her suffering. She was unconscious, all the sounds of her tormented body being merely the animal reactions of a system tortuously shutting down.

My father arrived, unkempt, shuffling, immediately prepared to "correct" the situation. "Where is she?" he asked in a loud voice, whose volume was prompted by his own deafness.

I felt my anger stirring, as if I could read his mind filled with accusations and old hurts. He had always assumed that his view of the world was the correct one, and he was unheedful of all who disagreed with him, forcing his listeners to hear his pronouncements, all conducted in a loud, often near-hysterical pitch, as if they were a verdict.

Somehow his deafness, brought on by age and by his years of exposure to the cacophonous din of a car factory, seemed to be an ironic counterpoint to those of us who wished that we could be deaf to his rants or unwanted counsel.

I used to watch his quarrels with my mother and view his flare-ups with me during my adolescence as a delirium that would pass only with his death.

Living with him was fraught with anxiety. We never knew where his impatience or anger would lead, or just what physical violence might suddenly erupt. As a child, I had once seen him slap my mother in the night, for what reason I never discovered, being too embarrassed and too frightened to ask. That sound remained a livid memory, and as his heavy, awkward old body now crumpled in the hospital wing, I felt an uneasy mixture of emotions towards him intermingling with my grief for my mother.

"Where is she? Can I see her?"

No, he was told, not yet.

"But why?" He had always disliked other people's injunctions.

He had obviously been roused from sleep, for his white hair was uncombed. The shirt he wore was stained by spilt food. His once strong, stocky body sagged. I had to hold him up. He grew concerned that he had forgotten to wear his dentures, and his lips seemed to pucker, his cheeks to be pulled hollow. His words were muffled and distorted, and he sometimes seemed to emit sucking sounds or clicks. He had forgotten, too, to wear his hearing aid, and I was particularly impatient because I was forced to repeat myself. Between spasms of grief and awkward self-consciousness about his missing dentures, he launched into a litany of regrets.

"Can she not hear us?" he asked, his dim eyes red-rimmed.

"I begged her not to smoke," he uttered in a half-sob. "I pleaded with her. I told her she was killing herself."

"This is not the time to go into all that!" I almost hissed.

"I want to say goodbye."

It was a normal desire, but of what sort of farewell was he capable in this bewildered state, without his dentures or his hearing-aid? Already his voice was raised too high in the room, and it competed with my mother's groans.

Was he thinking of asking her forgiveness? It could not free time or eradicate memory. It could not bring back love lost in the tides of their failed marriage. He could not nurture her now with confessions of his own mortality.

He wanted to kiss her even as her small body shook. He wanted to kneel by the bed, but his painfully swollen joints disallowed this, so he could do no more than bend over her grey head as I supported him.

For this simple moment, as the visible world was freezing outside, we were one family.

And I now wonder, years later, what thoughts and images flashed through my father's mind as he prayed her soul to rest. What grace could he expect for her when life had too often been a conspiracy against him, when it had abducted with an unceasing passion all the ones he loved? Was he thinking of his daughter he lost to cancer? Was he retreating even farther into the backward abysm of time and remembering his desperate mother in the desert? He used to invoke her name whenever he was ill or whenever deep in some private reverie. "Oh, mother!" he would groan. Once, in surgery in the middle of his life, he called for her out of his deep anesthesia. When his surgeon reported this, my mother said: "She died when he was a little boy. He barely remembers her."

The truth is I was angry that he had outlived her, that she had died betrothed to his name. She had died Lorna Constance Garebian. No more Alimo, no more the name of the mother. Her surname, because she had neglected to revert to her maiden name after their separation, would always be the name of the father.

His hospital grief had been disruptive to my mourning. Whatever the order or disorder, the structure or collapse of my emotions, he had to be reckoned as a part in that process. How death had kept the bond of his name ruthlessly to hers, how it could always remain in the center, a presence never marginalized.

"You are angry at your father," it was once suggested to me. "You are angry because he refuses to hear you."

I dropped my father off at his apartment, accompanying him to his front door where he fumbled with keys, trying to compensate for his poor eyesight by a practised touch. But at his age and in this emotional turmoil, he struggled with the safety-chain.

"Are you going to be all right?" I asked. "Try and sleep."

"I won't be able to sleep."

The apartment had been an empty shell ever since my mother separated from him after more than forty years of marriage. When they were together, through all the bruising years of nagging misgivings and the skirmishes of partners with disharmonious temperaments, at least the apartment was comfortable with the routines of hospitality. Now everything was uninviting.

The carpet was soiled with cigarette ash. The kitchen tap dripped. The air smelled musty.

My father refused to hire a cleaning lady. He had tried several, he claimed, but they were all unreliable and given to theft.

Loneliness had turned him paranoid. So many believed.

The truth is that he was always paranoid and fierce.

The night she died, I slept in her bed and felt a strange calm and soothing spirit.

Outside a blizzard suddenly erupted.

My mother had always hated cold and snow. Whenever she had to cross a street in winter, she would carry a little bag of sawdust which she scattered before her as a prevention against slipping. She had always been a dainty woman–sometimes comically so.

The blizzard could not cancel the memory of that daintiness.

How different her death was from my sister Elma's nine and a half years earlier, in June of 1981.

That death had moved me to compose poetry.

Even the stars have better fortune.
Are you counting their lights
As you sit among your sewn pictures in gold frames
The flowered ladies in Japanese gardens
Leaning under lacy snow
Distant hills
To take them outward
Upward
In light which is cool blue.
On the next wall
A young matador
Goring the bull
Whose thick body is a black cape
Writhing.
It is death in the afternoon.
You sit shadowed by these scenes
The light holding
The reins of your eyes
Now seeing too clearly
A presence, a wisdom
Eyes leaving prints on the room
While the rest of you becomes
A slow shadow
Fading
An echo without hardness.

My sister had died with a sudden shudder in June, 1981, cancer having swelled her like a gourd. She wanted to live, was never indifferent to the world from which she was slipping. Her mind moved in and out of chemic nightmare before they gave her cold Morpheus, and we tried to keep clear minds for farewells and accusations.

One of the last images I have of her alive: she is lying in bed, listening day and night to FM music. Her face is turned perpetually to the wall.

Death mask of my mother: she lies with her lips pulled too tightly across her mouth and appears to be grimacing. There is a dark patch on one of her hands that presses against the other, a rosary spilling out of this clutch.

The makeup must have worn off with mourners touching her.

Her dress was a beautiful blue silk with silver flecks.

If death is a journey, I am glad she wore blue.

Somehow it is easy to imagine that blue merging with the open, dry sky and a place to think towards.

And in my elegiac mood I remember Rilke. "Everywhere transience is plunging into the depths of Being."

The gruesome gone, the future is still not a road of stars. No words of whatever poem erase her dying, sound by sound. But her absence opens my text beyond a short, guilty comfort, turning it into a shapeshifter rebounding on myself.

My mother was a smiler. That is why her death-mask was so disturbing: it contradicted what I knew to be one of her distinguishing characteristics.

The smile is preserved in our family albums—even in the yellowing snapshots from the forties where in one badly framed image, with half her face cut off, she is holding me, a plump, happy toddler high on her hips, and smiling with a mother's pride—not decorative like a film star's, but true and pure as if that single clicking moment would stay golden like her baby's sun-kissed cheeks and free as his soft black curls.

And it is there, in a small hand-tinted Kodak photograph, in some Indian resort, where she poses in slacks before the profusion of leaf and bower in the same sunny era, with someone's shadow half insinuated into the picture.

And there again, decades later, under thin grey hair, in her son's suburban home, with her two grandchildren nestling in her dwindling arms. The smile has spread like a holiday joy from her small face to their almost cherubic ones, though the camera clicked while her eyes blinked, so what we see from beginning to end in that perennial moment is that open smile which softens the creases in her face.

And there again–this time rather tired–with family and friends at a dinner gathering, the dying daughter cut in half by the badly framed shot. She is second from the right as if the future were sucking her out of the scene after my sister, already half-vanished. And she is smaller than ever, like those sparrows that suddenly drop from the air in unbearable summer.

My elegy always returns to the father alive, to the ineffable source of my perpetual discomfort, the anarchic half of my double cosmos, because he will not cease to matter even when he himself is dead.

And so a reconstruction beyond despair?

But not before the vision of my own skin trembling, my own veil of darkness and evasion, the protection against uneasy memories. A personal earthquake of a lost mother and a predeterminedly lost father.

Now I see this as a ceremony, a broken taboo–because I have married memory to pain and to a text beyond my tribes.

My skin trembling is a price for being literary, for being a technician measuring unmapped territory.

This is not *terra firma*, this is not poised, precise. Whatever dry land is encountered, held dearly for personal use, pushes out of the wet, hidden "ground," wild and running everywhere under my skin.

Out of the blank, words come to dance in amazing circles.

Memory can never be progressive, only circular.

Whatever I do, whatever I remember, I descend or ascend in spirals, as time constricts the action, catching the mind alone in its spinning-wheel of grace and elegy.

She came to my teenaged son several times in bizarre dreams. In one she smiled, her small lined face in a subtropical rapture. "I'm back now!"

His anger shook her phantom: "Why don't you make up your mind? You're either dead or alive!" Then she vapourized, with her grey head sinking like a stone, her eyes going filmy.

He called this grotesquely wry dream a nightmare because he thought his grandmother's sudden dying was a betrayal of their mutual love.

A dream allows you to exist in two places at once. It bends the dreamer's mind and time as well.

But this was no consolation to my son, whose thin body was a reed, and whose heart quivered with even the feather-touch of her memory.

He was angry at her in his dream, and then felt a terrible guilt. He kept wanting to visit her grave every month, wanting to make some small offering–a rose, perhaps, or a prayer.

I remember the way he lingered at her body in the funeral parlour. I remember, too, the way he touched the edge of her coffin at the grave. It was a fingertip kiss. As if desperation had evaporated into lyric gentleness.

After the memorial prayers, the benediction, some further gesture would have broken the sun-shimmering silence of the winter air, in which all the other gravemarkers and their company of wreaths and vases kept a still vigil.

And in my eyes...

The grave's, indeed, a very private place. Under the lumps and clods of earth, beneath the careful rectangle, the geometry of burial is some hidden O.

I can sometimes feel that zero pulling my mind and its load of images.

My mother has died and I can now write about it.

But this is only part of what the text is made.

A TALE OF TWO CITIES

This could be a tale of two cities. One is Bombay, from which Mother came. Mumbai, the vernacular derived from *Maha Amba*, Great Mother. The other city wills itself nameless, from which my father fled wildly, running around all the edges of terror and rootlessness.

I can produce a clear, clean map of the first city, show you exactly where it lies in the dense tangle of a teeming subcontinent, show you how it suckles at the teat of Mother India. But what map should I give you of the second–the unnamed, disappearing trick of an atrocious magus, envoy to the underworld of inhumanity?

Call the first city a fabled dream, not because of inherent beauty, but because it is many-fabled, often lost in a plenitude of cheap illusion.

Call the second one a defacing nightmare, ever returning, an encircling *cauchemar* of history, scattering a tribe with reckless "SUDDENLY."

I am a divided river beneath a bizarre zodiac.

My father was Armenian–a traumatized survivor of this century's first holocaust–and my mother was Anglo-Indian, the tributaries of her blood flowing from two directions.

Even in Bombay, where I was born, I was never fully of a single place.

India and Armenia lie in a strange juxtaposition in my life. Yet, all is not as strange as it first appears.

My mother was Anglo-Indian, a mixed breed, but the original term signified an English gentleman or lady long-settled in India.

The first English woman to make a voyage to India in 1617 was actually the companion of an Armenian lady who had been born in India.

So the Armenians were in India long before the British. An Armenian merchant, Thomas Cana, landed on the Malabar Coast seven centuries before Vasco de Gama. He multiplied his wealth by trade in muslins and spices, thereby setting a course for fellow Armenian merchants, particularly in the age of Akbar the Great (1542-1602) which overlapped the Jacobean and Elizabethan eras. As traders, Armenians came to India by the overland route, through Persia, Afghanistan (once called Bactria), and Tibet. According to *Armenians In India*, by Mesrovb Jacob Seth, "It was Akbar, the Marcus Aurelius of India, who induced them to come and settle in his dominions instead of being mere sojourners in the country." A thriving community soon sprang up in Agra, where an Armenian church was erected in 1562. One of Akbar's *begums* was an Armenian, and so was the lady doctor in the royal Seraglio.

By the eighteenth century there were a number of wealthy merchants who made their influence felt, and there was even an Armenian version of Krupp in Lahore who cast great bronze guns, one of which was immortalized as "Zamzamah," a fire-breathing dragon in Kipling's *Kim*.

Armenians left their mark in Delhi, Surat, Kabul, Chandernagore, Julfur, Madras, Lucknow, and, of course, the large cities of Bombay and Calcutta. The largest Armenian community was in Calcutta, which accommodated three classes of Armenians: the so-called "Calcutta Armenians," whose ancestors had settled there in the 18th and 19th centuries, and most of whom enjoyed the benefits of English education; the "Julfa Armenians" from Ispahan, who settled late in the 19th century; and "Charmahalis" or emigrants of the early 20th century, who came from the Armenian villages of Charmahal in Persia.

Historical archives reveal some unforgettable characters. Sarmad, a merchant and Sufi poet during the reign of Emperor Shah Jehan, smoked *bhang* which he kept in an earthen pot near him always. He fell so passionately in love with a Hindu girl that in his distraction, he would go about naked in the streets. His indecent exposure finally earned him execution. Petrus Arathoon, another merchant, was employed by Lord Clive in the 18th century as a confidential agent in negotiations with Mir Jaffir for the overthrow of Suraj-ud-dowlah who had perpetrated the "Black Hole" tragedy. His services rendered, Arathoon went unrewarded and was eventually abandoned by Clive. There was the ignoble Carapiet Petrus Moorat, an importer who practised various impostures: surgeon, secretary to the Khedive's architect in Egypt, benefactor to young Armenian students (though his salary never exceeded twenty rupees a month), and scholar of the French and Armenian languages (though he spoke little French and no classical Armenian). And there was the eccentric Hripsimah Eleazar Leembruggen (the surname a result of marriage to a Dutchman in Surat), who was the soul of generosity but who was in the habit of drawing up a new will every year.

Armenians played important roles in various professions, including publishing. In South India two Armenian authors published groundbreaking works: in 1772 Shahamir Shahamirian printed the first work of Armenian political philosophy, whose author, Movses Baghramian, urged his people to awake from their "sleep and indolence," respond to European ideas, and end their exile from the motherland; and in 1773 Hakob Shahamirian published his book, a manual for the constitution of a democratic Armenia in the future.

Apart from Mesrovb Seth's book, there is, however, no extensive record of the entry, domicile, or collective Indian experience of the Armenians. There is abundant information on the English in India. There is even much information on the first English ladies on the subcontinent. As I read books on the subject, I see a faint shadow in the deep abysm of my mother's history.

MEMSAHIBS

They set out on the long voyage,
one ambassadorial ancestor having kissed the
   Moghul's toe,
with permission to "fish" in the Indian Ocean
and to set up a small trading post at Surat–
the Dutchman's unwanted scrap.
It was bait:
the Empire would survive their going
and India, used to their flicking tongues,
scandalized giggles and lazy scorn,
let them in–
a lure to the boredom that would
stun them,
these brittle *memsahibs*–
masters' wives–
untouchables in the dark loneliness,
among the rats and rabid dogs,
chintz-covered furniture mined by ants,
and English gardens wilting with decorum
between twelve and two
as well-groomed gentlemen called.
"Never shake hands with an Indian, my dear;
You never know where his hand has been,"
they'd laugh,
mosquitoes nipping at their ankles
and maggots slipping out of figs.
They'd had fair warning–
the shrivelled and dry "speculative ladies"
and the girls with a veneer to cover a "mental
   deformity"–

India was not for dabbling:
like the salt air
it could seep into your bones.
Still, they sailed,
biases billowing, with barbarous arrogance
into India's lasciviousness.
They wanted to shut the ocean
like a book
and land on Empire
clear of mutiny.
Under the winds' heavy petting
they tossed in their slight cabins
to the sea's heaving,
their right little, tight little voices
battered by the noise of wanton wave.
Used to the choreography of settled things
and not such insolence,
they endured,
sleeping, eating, passing their days in a thickening
stench,
worse off than Australian convicts
or scarecrow blacks on the Middle Passage.
There were minor diversions, rites of passage:
"crossing the line" before Neptune and transvestite
daughters,
and ports of call for tidy gardens, provisions, and
fresh water.
Such small pleasures for such a long journey,
where history was made with sea-washed eyes.

It was unpleasant for a "fishing fleet" lady to return to England unmarried. She would be stigmatized as a "returned empty."

The journey to India became safer and more pleasant in 1830, its locus charted by steamer between Suez and Bombay. A litany of sailing lines: Peninsular and Oriental, the Anchor and the Clan, Calcutta Star Line, the Rubatino. The trip acquired its own rules: where to sit on deck, what to wear, what to eat, when to have a game of quoits or shuffleboard.

"I do believe in dress and ease,
And fashionable dash.
I do believe in bright rupees,
And truly worship cash.

I do believe in marriage quite,
But don't believe in gents,
Unless you bind them pretty tight
By way of settlements.

I do believe entirely in
The Civil Service ranks:
The best are worth a deal of tin,
And none exactly blanks."

– "Arabella Green or The Mercenary Spin"
in *Lays of Ind*, 1875

What did they first see in Bombay, the Gateway to India? The bright waters of the Arabian Sea slapping the stone steps, vivid parrots shooting like small arrows in the azure, crows mixing in noisy riot, and Shiva's pigeons enjoying a gurgling convocation?

Beyond the stone-steps of dock, one sees the curving harbour and its green hills, white-washed villas and lush gardens–an Indian Bay of Naples.

Were they predisposed to denying that European association?

In their revolt against bullock-carts, veiled women daubed with caste-marks, black men all naked except for flimsy loin-cloths, and sun-stroked roads throwing up clouds of brown dust, the ladies–all decent, God-fearing Christians, at least to themselves–firmly entrenched themselves in their mental enclosures. India would be reduced, they assured themselves.

That had to be done for there simply was too much of everything, as one deep-rooted Anglo-Indian lady of the Victorian era remarked.

And she hadn't even witnessed the fabled extravagance of the *rajahs*, some of which was once described by Governor General Lord Auckland's sister in 1834:

> The first show of the day was [Ranjit Singh's Lion of the Punjab's] private stud. I suppose fifty horses were led past us. The first had emerald trappings, necklaces arranged on its neck and between its ears, and in front of the saddle two enormous emeralds, nearly two inches square, carved all over, and set in gold frames, like little looking-glasses.
>
> The crupper was all emeralds, and there were stud-ropes of gold hung on something like a martingale. The young rajah, Heera Singh, said the whole was valued at 37 lakhs but all these valuations are fanciful, as nobody knows the worth of these enormous stones; they are never bought or sold.
>
> The next horse was simply attired in diamonds and turquoises, another in pearls, and there was one with trappings of coral and pearl that was very pretty. It reduces European magnificence to a very low pitch.
>
> – EMILY EDEN'S DIARY,
> *UP THE COUNTRY*

The English were used to viewing Nature as a beneficent, tender Mother, but in India, this Mother changed both sex and disposition, becoming Siva, Lord of Change and Destroyer of Names and Forms. No matter how hard the invaders tried to subdue Siva, by bureaucracy or soldiery, they failed. Considering themselves princes and the Indians pariahs, they remained unable to penetrate its interior life and spirit. Most of these English males could be summed up in the image of the colonial with a *chota peg* in one hand, enjoying cigars, English music, billiards, and bridge at the club, while their women concerned themselves with amateur dramatics, garden parties, and *nimbupanis* (lime juice cordials) on the verandah at sunset, while assorted servants scurried about, attending to their whims or needs.

My mother's life as a married woman was very much like that of the English *memsahibs* in the nineteenth century, except that it was not a question of becoming a useful part of the Anglo-Indian community. My mother did not wish to keep India at arm's length, to look purely inward to the Anglo-Indian community for friendship, amusement, and security.

Dressing well, but not uncomfortably, was part of her duty as an Anglo-Indian housewife, and this meant keeping up to some degree with European fashions. There was nothing "native" about her dress, but nor was there anything extravagant. Her most stylish dress was a mauve velvet evening gown, following the contours of her body down to her ankle, and set off by a sash and velvet floweret. This she wore to dinner-dances, after bathing with Pear's soap, powdering herself with English talcum, and dabbing her neck, ears, and elbows (if I remember correctly) with Tosca 4711.

Shopping was done by taxi or victoria, although the daily supply of food was obtained by the full-time cook who undertook an early morning trip to Crawford Market by tramcar. I remember the evening ritual of taking up accounts with the cook in order to settle the expenses. Mutton, beef, and fish, each had its rate in annas. The meat came in large cuts, raw, red, marbled with fat and sinew. Brown, gnarled Bombay duck, high smelling and as chewy as cured leather, lay in heaps. Other fish (usually pomfret) lay with glassy eyes, whole and unscaled. Crabs, however, were received alive in our kitchen. They came in wicker baskets and once the lid was off, they could be seen scrabbling over one another, their pincers feeling the air, trying to find a way out of their enclosure. Any poultry, too, (usually a plump hen) was alive, squawking and fluttering its wings, though unable to thrash its legs which were firmly bound with cord. There would be an occasional partridge or quail, though not from the market; they came courtesy of Alvarez, a family friend, who would bring us a brace in a large coop.

When I write of these live birds, I can barely suppress a shudder, for I was a witness to their kitchen slaughter when Cook took his knife, sharpened on a grindstone, to their submissive throats, slitting them with a single firm action, then throwing their thrashing bodies onto the cold stone floor where they bled to death, the beatings of their wings ebbing ever more feebly second by second.

Huge pots of boiled water were readied in which to immerse their corpses so that Cook and Maid could then pluck the birds.

I can never forget the smell of blood, feathers, and raw flesh. Little wonder that I had no appetite for curried chicken in those days.

My mother also bought two hens, thinking that the least she would get from this modest purchase would be fresh eggs and, perhaps, a few chicks which could later multiply the egg production. The hens were stored in a specially made coop in our passageway leading to the kitchen, but in the morning the birds were led down the backstairs, a spiral metal staircase, to the dusty yard where they could scratch and peck at worms or scattered grains, exercise their clucks, strut their stuff, and return at dusk like two fine ladies after a day's leisurely ramble. Cook coaxed them upstairs, but they insisted on roaming through part of the house before making their lackadaisical way to the coop where they would settle quietly for the night.

They gave me the shivers, not because they were aggressive, but because I nursed an innate phobia of birds, dating back to the time when I was traumatized at the age of four or five at Crawford

Market when my godfather flung a full-grown hen at me in order to to stop my whines and cries in the backseat of the family car. I had thought I was being attacked by a bird of prey, because, although the bird's feet were tightly bound by string, its wings were free to flutter in frenzy, and its angry squawks scared the daylights out of me. Ever since then, I was never able to be in the presence of a winged creature without turning cold and clammy.

ANIMAL SLAUGHTER

Bombay conditioned me to witnessing the slaughter of animals. I once saw a pig being killed in the farmyard for a feast-day dinner at a Catholic seminary. A single bullet was used to stun the animal, and as soon as it fell, the slaughterer slit its throat with a knife as other men grabbed its feet. Gouts of dark blood dropped into the dust.

I was accustomed to witnessing goats killed for Mohammedan festivals:

a portentous hush
as the slaughterer's knife
divides the creature in the light:
sinews relax
in the trespass musing
on the air's strange sweetness
the blade makes confident music
sibillant with slashes.
The day is so clear it is unclean
this act, a ritual.
A place of darkness, the sticky
smell of heat
reflected on beige walls.
These, and the figure stretched

like a live carpet
under the holy executioner's feet.
A sharp hot stink of muscle and fat
dwindling body   blood
filling the mud pit
the goat's eyes look on darkness
with a deepening greyness.
I have seen some truth in the throes
of prostration, some bloody truth
of sacrifice & human need
–in the skin tearing in long flaps
and rummaged bowels
hissing guts fall
in squirming facts
upon the ground,
proving a small relation
one more truth
between two disorders
–mine (for seeing) &
the creature's loss of life
spurting through frothy jaws
in the centre of a voyeur's circle.
Now its presence is known by absences
the hollow of a body
dark hole in the neck
separated ribs
men shall live well after Ramadan
their days and nights cornucopias of flesh
falling fruit in a short journey to oblivion.
Down to the nervous marrow of my bones
There's something in this richness that I hate.

WATER, *HIJRAS*, AND MIXED CODES

As a Cancerian, water is my element. And there was much of it in Bombay, a schizophrenic bejewelled slum built on a peninsula that was an imperial dowry in a European marriage.

Fishermen were here long before the English. There were, in reality, seven islands: Worli, Mahim, Salsette (once a Portuguese walled city), Matunga, Colaba (formerly noted for European cotton presses and a military cantonment), Mazagaon, and Bombay. Long before the British joined them, turning part of the sea into land, and confusing cartographers who were never sure where sea had been before the land.

Maps were unreliable.

The goddess Mumbadevi–with variable names, Mumbabai, Mumbai–presided over the sea. Then the Portuguese came and named the place Bom Bahia for its harbour where they sought to shelter their merchant and war ships. Bombay passed into English hands only through marriage, when Catharine of Braganza had to offer it up to Charles II of England as her dowry.

But the sea remained itself.

"The sea is aristocratic in Bombay," wrote Dom Moraes in his Indian journal, *Gone Away*. "The sea is aristocratic in Bombay, lying under the lighted windows of rich houses, purring to itself and listening to the subdued thunder of cocktail-shakers from within. If the sea were not there, one felt, there would be no parties."

I remember the sea, drunk with its own power, spewing against the rocks that sometimes smelled like lava. I remember, too, the parties by the sea, parties in Colaba where the inevitable male film star was coaxed into making love to himself in an imaginary romantic movie for booze-sodden voyeurs.

Or parties on Madh Island where the gentle grotesque, Jiji Goldstein–a professional wrestler (former Greco-Roman Olympian from Rumania), married to a diminutive South Indian spitfire–was teased into mock-grappling with the company clown, a man whose wife had run off to Europe with a foreign lover, and whose own comic party-piece of mimicked foreign accents gave no consolation to his riven heart.

Parties where Ali, the adulterous Muslim family man, indulged his Christian paramour with displays of ostentatious flattery before returning to his wife in *purdah* in the humble domesticity of a modest tenement. Or parties where the latest arrivant from Nuffield or Sheffield or Kent or London was showered with sycophancy simply because of his accent. Parties where bottles of illicit liquor–the product of the grossest fermentation in rubber hot-water-bottles buried in sand–were a surrogate sacramental until the customary raid by C.I.D. officers eager to be perceived as zealous upholders of the Prohibition laws of urine-drinking Morarji Desai. The raids brought panic to the women, avid curiosity to the children, and studied nonchalance to the men who usually managed to flush the incriminating evidence down the toilet and fling the bottles into the refuse heap conveniently located behind the house.

Bombay taught me that there was little that nature really abhorred.

Bombay had a community of *hijras* or eunuchs. I saw a few of them wandering around Bellasis Road, though a larger number prowled the sands of Chowpatty Beach. They were notorious, the subject of lurid rumours. Many started off as children of prostitutes or as beautiful boys mutilated for sexual gratification. Dressed in *saris*, adorned with bangles, necklaces, and earrings, they were treated as deviants consigned to an underworld of vice. They were prey to particularly perverse homosexuals who liked to inflict pain on their paid "slaves." However, they did have a positive symbolic role. *Hijras* were valued for their role as dancers at weddings and naming ceremonies, for their blessings would lead, it was believed, to further fertility.

Bombay incarnated contradiction.

The house we lived in faced St. Anthony's Home, an orphanage for babies and children abandoned by those who had forced them into the world. It was widely known that newborn babies were frequently laid at the front door of St. Anthony's, to be quietly accepted by the convent nuns who ran the place. It was also widely rumoured that most of these babies were the offspring of neighbouring prostitutes, the dark, shameless wantons, at trellised windows, who called openly to customers on Falkland Road, a stone's throw from the orphanage. Many of the whores had started off as children abducted or bought from families in Nepal, Assam, and Kashmir. Customers valued hairless genitalia, but if the virgins proved difficult, they were left to the expertise of professional rapists. Sex and religion had a virtually symbiotic relationship. The babies were baptized as Catholics and reared to be well-mannered youth. Girls, of course, were tutored to become young brides; the homely ones consigned to a fate of further prayer and meditation as potential nuns.

I went to school with shy Indian princes and randy sons of sheikhs who cultivated a repertoire of filthy jokes in which pederasty and bestiality were common themes. I went to school with Iranis who worshipped fire and Zoroaster, and Parsis who, like them, gave their dead to the vultures of the Towers of Silence. Some of our favourite gossip was about the drive up Malabar Hill, from whose height an occasional finger or scrap of human flesh would fall onto your windshield. I never actually experienced any such thing, but it was a wonderfully macabre piece of gossip to spread to overawed visitors.

Another bit of morbid exaggeration concerned the Hindu custom of cremation, for it was rumoured that the priest would have to beat the corpse down in its pyre as the muscles of the deceased contracted, causing the body to rise involuntarily like a zombie determined to haunt the living. The truth had a different significance: the custom of breaking the skull was supposed to facilitate the departure of the soul through an opening in the body.

I went to school where Francisco, a Goan boy stammered for three years in the same grade; he talked and smiled so relentlessly to himself that he seemed destined for an asylum. A school where

Ashok Sathe, a precocious boy read Ezra Pound's Cantos for leisure, and where another, Dom Moraes, was soon to become the youngest winner of the Hawthornden Prize for Literature. I went to school with a boy whose mother was gunned down by her estranged lover, propelling the boy into a nervous tremor that never left him. There was another boy, French, with curly hair the colour of grain, and with eyes a blue chevron, whose grandmother, it was said, had once run the most exclusive brothel in Bombay.

I went to school with Higgins, a gawky Anglo-Indian, who habitually masturbated in dark cinemas, and who fantasized about seducing the most voluptuous mothers of his peers.

I went to school with others like myself, not quite in the Indian vein, though not at all certain of their true style.

My boyhood was one of mixed codes, and to those not born in India it sometimes sounds like a fabrication, a sequence of invented gestures or lies.

Truth and fiction are often improperly categorized. Fiction is a name that sometimes describes the failure of your critic's imagination.

THIS QUEST IS NO ROMANCE

This quest is no romance. There are no notorious family "characters," no funny scandals. All the gestures are true, not imagined. All the ghosts are quietly haunting.

If this were fiction, I would begin with the odd Victorian house in a compound of bizarre architectural mixtures. The compound, called "The Retreat" in virtually ironic counterpoint to the polyglot tumult of amazing ethnic relationships, was set only yards away from the badly potholed street, and was a dusty cluster of bungalows, villas, two-storeyed residences with wooden balustrades, wrought-iron verandah-railings, and either conical or squat roofs. It was a chaos of bastard styles, a grotesquely comic legacy of British colonialism.

Plots of papaya, guava, plantain, and green mango trees were rough territorial boundaries for the houses, and they were freely raided by the compound children, boldly unmindful of the spying eyes behind bamboo blinds. There were also fig trees and a wild mulberry bush for those who dared risking scarred fingers while reaching past thorns for slightly sour berries.

Hawks circled and cried in their midair copulations, as chattering crows and brown sparrows, serenading tom-cats and foolishly strutting poultry thickened the textures of sound.

The houses formed three sides of the oblong compound with a huge rusting gate, never closed, as the fourth side. At the compound's rear sprawled small huts, derelict garages, congested godowns that housed poorer classes, and a deep well covered and painted white, which became the object of old wives' tales spun to frighten children into staying away from it.

The huts had corrugated tin roofs which set up a metallic clatter whenever the rains fell. Dark and smoky within, with several emaciated Hindu occupants coughing away on *bidis* as groundnut oil cooked on primus stoves, the huts had cool cow-dung spread and dried at the doorways, and on this aromatic carpet were set intricate patterns in coloured chalk powder, many variations of a mandala, each configuration a testament to an insistent urge for beauty pushing its way through poverty of means.

The garages had the Goans, all wiry and rampant with children, the parents squabbling, the offspring squalling, all reduced to a decadent nostalgia for a home-place still occupied by the Portuguese.

Marwaris and Muslims took to the godowns. Better dressed and with healthier physiques–certainly more glistening skin–than their immediate neighbours, they were the quietest, most private of the three groups–except for wedding days and feast days when they rivalled the Hindus and Goans for festive noise and gaudy accoutrement. So private were they that I did not know for years that the neatly-dressed, smilingly polite family man, with camera slung over one shoulder, was, in fact, a brothel-owner and not a professional photographer.

They all lived beside garbage heaps and in a bustling communality, and as they washed their pots and pans, did their meagre laundry on flat stone slabs, and pitched the dirty water an arm's length from their doorways, streams ran dark and muddy at the rear of the compound.

They were within "The Retreat" but not really a publicly acknowledged part of it. They were simply the inevitable embarrassment, a fact of life in a city bursting with pluralities. They were a shadow-world, denizens whose will to survive was as strong as their squalor.

When people spoke of "The Retreat" what they meant were the middle-class houses of accountants, store-owners, teachers, public administrators, superannuated widows, et cetera.

As Scots novelist Andrew O'Hagan puts it, a childhood home seems to exist for nobody but you. It is "a mythic address, not chosen by you."

There were palpable characters in "The Retreat." They are chiefly ghosts now, moving only as shadows on this page. Ghostly presences, generators of my ambivalences to their manifold stories. They can be small pieces of a narrative to which I would trust this memoir.

My writer's hand holds itself out to their traces, and no matter how strange their presences, how unfinished their stories, they become a tentative extension of me.

I want to reduce the affliction of certain determinations.

In the vastness of India, it made sense to hold on to a smaller scale, a tractable idea of oneself.

My father had a wide circle of acquaintances and customers. They included surgeons and physicians (one of them an expensive quack who once prescribed a mild dilution of arsenic as a cure for my premature grey hair), high court judges, journalists (including two brothers who wrote some of the most graceful cricket commentary this side of Neville Cardus), lawyers, symphony orchestra conductors (including Zubin Mehta's father who was encouraged by my father to send his son to Europe), actors and actresses (many of whom cultivated pseudonyms to conceal their modest roots). We knew that the Soares sisters who lived directly below us were related to Merle Oberon who pretended she was born in New Zealand and did not want anyone to discover that her London maid was her own mother. We took a perverse delight when Oberon's glamorous face required heavy pale makeup on screen to lighten her dark complexion. Her accent, too, gave her away–at least to our minds–for it it was just carefully English enough to sound cultivated rather than natural.

Our neighbours ranged from Khorshed Irani, a bone-thin seamstress, who had once trained to be a commercial artist and who gave me my first formal art lesson with oils; Nissim Ezekiel, a poet and playwright; his brother, Hannan, an economist much cherished by universities in the States; and Priscilla Soares, nicknamed "Doc" because she had once practised medicine, who drove her car without benefit of a license. When stopped by a policeman for a minor traffic violation, she feigned astonishment at being required to show her papers: "Officer, I didn't know I needed a license to drive now that I'm retired."

One of Doc's younger sisters, also a spinster, was Kitty, a patient, soft-spoken seamstress, who took a liking to me as a child and entertained me with tales about *shikars*, *machans*, and man-eating tigers and who promised to make a leather Tarzan loincloth such as the one worn by Johnny Weismuller. I thought I would assist her by drawing a human figure, replete with body parts, and adding a caution: "You know, Aunt Kitty, those two dots at the top of the body are not buttons."

"The Retreat" had its share of curiosities: Mrs. Davidson, gnarled with age and arthritis, with hands shaped like talons; her daughter, Edie, a professional spinster with a rather peculiar lady friend nicknamed "Buffy" from Simla who dressed like a man in tweed suits, puffed on cigars, and spoke in a deep voice; old Mrs. Saldanha, hobbling around on bunioned, pigeon-toed feet, but full of risible anecdotes, trivial gossip, and Catholic homilies; Khodi Irani, the urbane owner of Golden Wafers (the best potato chips I have ever tasted), but a disillusioned alcoholic who turned to varnish when he ran out of booze and died in his thirties; Dhubi and Temeena, sisters who lived with their extended family in a long white villa, and who had (in addition to a playboy bachelor-brother and another, saintly brother, the St. Francis of the block, who fed breadcrumbs daily to the twittering sparrows) the dumbest, most handsome golden retriever imaginable and two aging cockatoos in splendid gilt cages, from where the birds whistled at visitors, mimicked voices and then gurgled with laughter at their own jokes; and, best of all, Mr. and Mrs. Jamshedjee, the epitome of Bombay colonials.

Mr. Jamshedjee was a tall, sturdy figure even in old age. He had retired from the British India civil service but remained a thorough Anglophile. Clad in white with a khaki sunhat or *topi*, he would saunter forth, cane in hand, in the noonday sun, like mad dogs and Englishmen in Noel Coward's lyric. Although he and his wife were Parsis and spoke Gujerati at home, the pair read only English newspapers, hoarding the back editions so that all their rooms smelled of old paper. Although she was well past the aid of cosmetics, Mrs. Jamshedjee owned an ornate dresser with three mirrors. Eighty years after Queen Victoria's death, she assiduously preserved all her Victorian furniture.

Every evening at 7 p.m., they would step into the compound, set out two deck chairs, and commence their ritual. Old Mr. Jamshedjee would crank the His Master's Voice gramophone while his wife fanned herself with a hand *punkah*. The couple were obsessed with John Phillip Sousa and British marches, although their repertoire opened with "Rule Britannia" and concluded with "God Save The King."

The margins of "The Retreat" held other fascinations. There was a vigorous, red-haired Pathan who had once sliced a Hindu with a knife during a quarrel. There was a Goan family of seven crowded into a smoky godown, their eldest daughter, a nubile thing of fifteen, betrothed to a paunchy, middle-aged bachelor but yearning at night for her secret, teenaged beloved. I witnessed the spectale when her Romeo had to clamber down from the roof, pursued by her irate father and his two sons armed with staves and brooms.

My favourite memories of the "characters" from my childhood are of my godfather, Charles Ronald Williams, my father's bachelor-friend, once a cargo clerk. He was a large man with thick hands and feet, a lump the size of a small egg above one ear, a dark, round, smiling face, and hair that was forever grey at the temples. His nickname was "Billy," carved, no doubt, out of his surname, and he was charming company, especially to children, whom he always surprised with candy or chocolates and many jokes. He was open fun, even when slightly drunk, though my mother ultimately felt that he visited us too frequently and monopolised my father's time. She resented the fact that my father played up to Bill whenever he visited, and when she nagged at my father, Bill would intervene with a light grimace: "Oh, Lorna, stop making kitkit." That was his Indian-English equivalent for "complaining."

He was Billy to us, children, Billy who did exact and comic impressions of foreigners and dancing eunuchs, Billy who promised me a real windfall after his death. "And what will that be?" I asked with wide eyes. "All the palm trees along Juhu beach." Somehow it did not matter that this was pure exaggeration, even an outright lie. There was charming roguery in the manner in which he spun out my expectation. He was a fund of wonderful stories, usually told against himself. He had a lightly wicked sense of self-satire, as when he proudly boasted of his European legs–European because they were lighter in colour than his face and arms exposed to the Indian heat.

One of my early fascinations was with the coloured tattoo on his right forearm. It was of a naked woman who would wiggle and gyrate every time he'd contort his forearm. He also had a tattoo of a majestic eagle, but it was the nude woman that caught and held my eyes. When I was a young boy, I never associated the figure with carnality; it was parlour entertainment and fascinating to behold, rather like the flip books where photographs or illustrations could be brought to animated life by a mere flip of the left thumb from back to front, and with your right from front to back. As I blossomed into adolescence, I saw the tattoo differently, as an anomaly of something wicked and slightly freakish. And Bill himself fell outside my immediate sympathy, for he was so loyal to my father as to be considered by me as someone on the other side of my trust. I became his critic, still appreciative of his charming roguery, yet not altogether convinced of his complete sincerity as a family friend. After all, was he my father's friend simply because he was liberally plied with food and drink at our house, given financial assistance whenever he so much as hinted at its need, and comforted on rare occasions when he was in low spirits?

If I were to make a proper story out of the material of his life, I would end it with my rejection of him. I celebrated his mirth and laughter, enjoyed his social company, while my mind composed a critical judgement of the quality of his friendship. Then, as he stuck to my father as close as ever, even when it was time for us to leave India, I wanted to get rid of him, and it did not work. I would go on with my life, and yet he would never really melt away.

These characters made for a "storied" past. What I have written are mere traces in their memory.

Inside our house, the floor tiles glistened a morocco red. In the monsoon season, the air was a choking dampness, and the bed-linen sucked up this moisture so that you always awoke damp and felt a little soiled.

The hottest months were a perpetual furnace into which we walked like fated creatures. The houses had huge ceiling fans, but these were often futile against the shimmering humidity. A sparrow that accidentally strayed into the circuit of the fan-blades would fall decapitated onto the tiles.

In the hottest months, our bodies broke out into rashes and prickly heat. And as the insects collected for their bloodthirsty invasions, our beds were draped with heavy mosquito nets "stranded in the air like the dresses of hanged brides."

Our house was vast. The living-room had no conventional ceiling but its corners seemed to soar into a crowning turret, a cathedral ceiling profaned by audacious sparrows that tucked their nests and young into any crevice, unmindful of the broad-armed fans that guillotined many of their errant brood.

Other intruders were sometimes sonar-defective bats that flitted in their prehistoric ugliness, sometimes brushing against our ears. We children screamed with superstitious fear that a flittermouse would grapple itself to one of our precious ears, never to be pulled away, unless it also tore off a flap of skin while siphoning off our blood in its death-throes. When servants and adults mounted a concerted attack against the invaders by closing all doors and swinging against the flapping creatures with brooms, we children protected our ears and made more than enough noise to harrow the dead.

My Bombay boyhood was dense with sound. In the first reticence of dawn, roosters crowed the city awake. And in the sunburst of church bell, families clattered with their rousings. Cooks fanned kitchen-fires into a morning crackle, maids slapped cutlery and crockery into place on tables, cars started, buses wheezed, tramcars clanged or creaked around street corners, and children dressed indolently for school while mothers and *ayahs* urged them on stridently.

When it rained, which it did for multitudinous days and nights, the rain went from a poignant spattering to an insane flooding, before trembling itself into submission. Mail slots clicked open and envelopes thudded onto stone floors. Vendors began their urgent pitches as maids' coal-glowing irons hissed over cottons and linens. The iceman staggered up flights of stairs, heaving blocks wrapped in sackcloth, and the waterman bore huge bladders of fresh water that went gushing and gurgling into empty metal barrels. Cleaning women scraped and scratched at residues of dirt on wall and floor, and used crude whisks, brooms, and brushes for daylong labours as stray dogs barked for scraps and at strangers. In the ghettos, the women pounded and rolled herbs and spices on slabs of stone, or beat out the soapy water from sodden clothing before rinsing and hanging the pieces to dry in the sun.

At school, bells divided the day into regulated compartments of time and learning, though we always preferred the special recess and lunch bells that freed us from the tedium of class and released us into the schoolyard where freewheeling hawks circled, calling to one another before swooping to snatch a sandwich out of an unsuspecting hand. The playground was a din of feet against footballs or cricket bats whacking and cracking hard red balls into the outfield or shouts from the volleyball and basketball courts crowded with leaping and lunging bodies and a blur of legs.

A peculiarity of the sounds of my boyhood was the polyglot nature of the human noise. Bombay was a conglomeration of ethnicity–a mosaic of race, religion, colour, and language–and its languages, spoken in a variety of pitches, registers, ranges, and shadings, were a rich babel to those beyond their contours. I spoke little Hindi, less Marathi, no Gujerati, Sanskrit, Urdu, Arabic, or Konkani, so my linguistic decrepitude outside my mother tongue gave me small claim to the accessible Indian world. A person risks real ignorance at times for the sake of unilingual imperialism.

"The Retreat," Bellasis Road, Byculla. The naming gives comfort, makes palpable what could simply be a figment of a re-imagined past.

It was a house into which my parents moved sometime after they were married in April, 1942.

MARRIAGE PORTRAIT

My parents' marriage portrait is sober and formal, having been done in a studio with dark curtains and painted backdrops, and by a camera on a tripod, where the photographer would suddenly duck under a black cloth to pop a flashbulb. There is no spontaneity in the picture, the photographer having been overly practised in posing couples. My parents stand facing the camera squarely. They look surprisingly solemn after the nuptials, as if holding their breath in case they blur the camera's focus.

Or are they holding their breath for a recondite reason? My mother, her white skin turning her even younger than her twenty years, shows a stiff formality with none of the aura one associates with a wedding. Her train spreads like a pool of white water, and some of the sprays and flowers from her bouquet seem to drip into that pool. My father looks starchily confident and not at all cheerful. Could he have cowed her like a nineteenth century Victorian husband taking possession of one more collectible? Or is he simply overwhelmed by his good luck–the present gleaming with conjugal promise more palpable than the Ararat of his aborted boyhood?

Or are they both simply getting the marriage off to a serious start?

Does she have a premonition of his paranoia or violence? Does she know where his mind is, in whatever well of memory he would always search for the rest of his life?

Impossible to tell from this portrait what the two thought of love. And yet as a newly-wed couple, they must have looked into each other's face with eyes that kissed.

1942 and the war was not yet over.

War would never be over for him.

The day when church-bells sang out for their vows, and the night when he moved toward her with a plunging ardour were only a pause–a miraculous eclipse of darkness.

This was civilization at last. Far enough for comfort from Yerevan or Beirut, from hump-backed caravans, from marauding Turks and Kurds, from tides of chaos.

I can look into his wedding-day eyes...and so I am present in that picture, submerged in my parents' lives, in a plot that now stretches back over five decades filled with phrases from remembered moments.

What kept him alive for this moment? He had no special skill for remembering towns on a map. Ancestral faces were washed away from his mind, and every hot wind–it must have been the *Samiel* from Turkey, poison mixed with air–burned away the sand crossings, the prints of human caravans and corpses.

All Europe was fighting a war on three continents, but in his orphaned boyhood, where was Europe when survival was mostly a ghost of a chance, like water slipping through weak fingers?

My father never had a fully-named world. He had no maps to fix civilization in place. War made him an amnesiac. There were always dangers and secrets about him. He was always a patient who never fully recuperated.

He couldn't name most ancestral names though he wanted to breathe love into the winds that would blow towards Ararat. He couldn't even see their faces among the remembered willows or the mountain flowers, and when he looked at the moon it mirrored only a tangle of shadows.

"NO STORY IS EVER TOLD ONCE"

For almost four decades I have not lived in my birthplace, though even when I did, my nightmare was that I would never leave but be trapped like a land in drought.

Every summer my Mississauga garden lies in a blaze of heat, but without the frantic noise of insects and birds, yapping dogs, screeching cats, and the calls of dusty vendors from that other ancient place.

As I write these short bursts of reflection, the morning passes–its shadows flitting like the clouds across hills.

What was it like growing up with elephants pressing in slow motion through streets or with snakes slithering into secret tunnels under porches?

It was never really like that, my Anglo-Indian childhood, and in order to vanquish the rumours I need to be as precise as a stethoscope.

"No story is ever told once." – MICHAEL ONDAATJE

My father told his story repeatedly, and yet it was never really the same. With each repetition, there was some expansion, some embellishment, or some alteration which seemed to come from an imagination other than his own.

Could he have been prompting me out of my sullen refusal to believe him? Could he have been prophesying that his story would be told again–by me, the unwilling harbourer of his ghosts?

Three deaths made me a voyager: first, my sister Elma's; next, my mother's a decade later; and then, my father's. Each death made me sink into a labyrinth of remorse, tangled memories, and a fierce determination to piece together the chaotic pieces of a family history. Not to make a tidy mosaic but at least a montage of gestures and traces before I myself am finally invaded by death, when I become its quarry and not simply its voyeur.

THE ALIMOS

My mother's smiles remind me that on her side, we are a family of smilers. In almost every Alimo photograph, my relatives look at the camera and smile, even if one-quarter of the shot is plunged in shadow. They smile out of the shadows. And these are not artificial grins, created only for the camera lens; the cheerful lips break out of a luxury of feeling, as if no matter what the season or stress under the skin, there is something to lighten the mood. Better that the air around us not be permitted to become heavy and settled.

All of my uncles and my aunt, my mother and hers, all know that their smiles will carry some message about life, about even so ordinary a thing as a guava tree or a little red mulberry, or, perhaps, Uncle "Tiger's" scheme for a night of roisterous fun, or Aunt Pat's expectation of her young knight on his shining motorbike, appropriately named a Triumph, roaring through the oppressive heat to carry her off to an imaginary life.

My grandfather, patriarch of what would have been a tribe of seven, is content with what he has bred. How firmly he hugs young Reginald to him, the youngest of his children, as if the boy should one day know, too, just like his father just what it takes to be the head of a family.

And my grandmother, diminutive, plump, her dark hair beginning to recede, her pencil-slim eyebrows carefully plucked, her lips highlighted, she holds in her smile the benediction of something starting, perhaps even before the war abroad comes to an end, that beginning being in the weddings she foresees for her two daughters.

I remember her sagging breasts and heavy belly, short legs bent like bows, round shoulders and fleshy arms. In essence, she was a summary of curves, softly assertive rather than carnally provocative, and she gleamed with good humour.

I was frequently taken on visits to her home in Parel, where she lived with her second husband, a displaced Englishman named Ken Face whose skull had been bashed by rioters during the Quit India movement. She couldn't stay still. While he listened intently to the BBC radio for county soccer and cricket scores, she just had to refill my glass of pop or hurry to serve more homemade savouries or cake. And whatever my mother reported of my mischief or innocence, she found amusing, emphasizing her delight either in a high laugh or a cheerful giggle. I don't think she was aware that her laughter was sometimes too high or that she smiled too much or that she plied her visitors with refreshments even when they didn't want any more. Hospitality to her meant a perpetual offering of food, drink, and mirth. She would, if she could, have offered me the world.

In many respects, she was like everybody's grandmother who, even more than his own mother, would grant him unconditional love. The sort of protectress with whom you felt you were communicating in a special way even when you didn't speak. The sort of guardian angel who was real, whose breath was warm and sweet like honey, who would never let you suffer indignities or nightmares.

And yet, of course, every other boy's grandmother could hardly be like your own, the one who is palpably connected to your childhood, whatever its weather, grievings or celebrations, mischiefs or punishments. You can see your jokes brightening in her eyes, her small plump body twitching with laughter.

Despite the smiles, the family names trail off, even on the more familiar Anglo-Indian side: Ewart Alimo and Nellie Margaret (*née* De Mello), my maternal grandparents; Patricia, Lorna, Valentine, Edmund ("Tiger"), and Reginald, the offspring that survived as railway children, for Ewart worked for the British India railway.

There were two other children, a boy and a girl, who had not survived childhood, and beyond their christening names, they were a vanished memory.

Lorna, Valentine, and Reginald are now also gone. Valentine (nicknamed "Sunny" for his gentle, sweet, bright disposition) was the first to go–a victim at twenty-six of spinal meningitis on his first wedding anniversary in London, just as he had new-found happiness through a wife who had been his childhood sweetheart; Reginald, the youngest and frailest son, found Birmingham too cold and grey for his weak lungs. Exhausted by the rigours of work, overly-prolific fatherhood, and an England in which he shrank into working-class poverty gilded only by the sentimental myth of hearth and home.

I remember little of my three uncles, except for "Tiger's" harum-scarum activities. Short but muscular, he had aspirations to be a professional boxer, but he preferred to loaf around town rather than train assiduously, and it was common for him to be on the town all day, race home, gobble a quick meal, and dash off to the boxing arena just in time for his contest.

The only story I can recall of Reggie is the one related by my mother about his appearance as a fairy in a school production of *A Midsummer Night's Dream*, where, settling comfortably on a perch in the set, he pulled off his socks and fell asleep, apparently charmed by Shakespeare.

And "Sonny," the soft young gentleman, left behind a self-portrait in pencil, a few letters, photographs, and affecting memories for his mother and siblings of his all too brief life.

With the almost inevitable scattering of the dispossessed and the final dwindling by death, there is only Aunt Pat (with her pseudonym, Patricia Parr) who can provide traces of relationships in my ancestry. But she is still recovering from a stroke that plucked out many family stories by the root, leaving her a thin harvest of random memories.

Aunt Pat, the tough one, petite in stature, bruised in heart and mind, yet relentless in her urge to salvage meaning in the family romance. Only, her meaning is really a fierce compulsion to justify a secure place for the Alimos in the hectic of time. She had battled her parents so that she could live her life without their interference or approval, even though this had meant marrying a man of impressive muscle but less impressive integrity, and even though this had meant battling her in-laws to a standstill in Jubbulpore, a town forever on the verge of wilderness. She was always a battler who seemed to relish her own reputation for pugnacious independence. Inappropriately nicknamed "Dolly,"–a nickname she loathed–she was the natural defender of her siblings when they were threatened by bullies. She could shinny up a tree as quickly as any boy, and she packed a powerful wallop. Where my mother, two years her junior, entertained herself with dolls, mimed playing the piano on a settee and singing to them, Pat was out playing football or hockey, riding bicycles, and stealing fruit from an orchard without getting caught. She must have resented my mother at times for being their father's favourite. He had, after all, nursed Lorna when she suffered from rheumatic fever in her teens.

I understand from my aunt's letters to me that my mother exploited this favouritism at times. The sisters wore identical dressess–an unfortunate practice among certain middle-class families–and when my mother spilt food on hers, she would slyly wear one of her sister's, until Pat found out. Then all hell would break loose, with Pat's tearing a collar in anger.

Pat's aggressiveness gave her a sometimes false layer of cruel hardness or bristling contrariness. In reality, she is a generous person, ever willing to help those friends in true need, whether this takes the form of house-cleaning duties for them or suggesting remedies for aches and pains, all the way from lentils and sunflower oil to boiled green papaya, a West Indian remedy for high blood pressure ("You dice it, remove seeds, and boil till pulpy, then drink a cupful every day."). So, why, I wonder, is her blood pressure up again? She is adamant: "Now it is up again due to harrassment of ground floor tenant and inaction on part of the Council, so every form I get from the Council I tell them what I think of them. ...I will write to the P.M. again." She has always been true to herself. But harmony eludes her. In her old age in London, she rails more often than she should, finding fault with the government, foreign policy, the town council, socialized medicine, recalcitrant neighbours.

My mother's side can be charted back to England and, perhaps, even to Spain, Portugal, or Ireland. It is a side seduced by Europe and pretending a bond to that wife of many cultural marriages, though family members who have gone "home" to England have usually inherited little beyond disillusionment and a weary resignation to the idea of being a prodigal detached from Anglo-Indian history. The English, dispossessed of imperial grandeur, have eyed them with misgivings.

Memory invades those who are old
But forgetfulness is the stronger invader.
They have forgotten where they are, what they have
lost
Beyond the plagues of snakes and *fakirs*
The beggars littering dung-encrusted roads
The whores with painted faces inviting
Secular love in waves of heat
The green hills terraced with tea
Caves covered with erotic graffiti
The high silhouettes of coconut palms

And anarchy of wild flowers.
England makes them want to remember
Their traces in the solitude of high noon
The heavy monsoon
The raw beauty scavenged by Empire.

MONSOON

The monsoon, a word I can never forget, that breeds images of natural violence. Leslie Forbes, in her rich novel, *Bombay Ice*, which happens to have the best literary evocation of Bombay in my experience, presents vivid pictures of an Indian monsoon. My mind floats over her words, trapping some, and I make a net of poetry:

there was water
holding the land hostage
before cartographers and maps
the seven islands emerging
unwillingly from seven seas
reinventing geography
as if those islands were visions
of real cities
and as those cities grew
insular
the peninsula was seen
shaped like a hand, pulling
itself from the sea
which still dreams of phosphor eyes
drowned sailors
as the *dhows* drift
their boatmen deep-lidded at sunset.
water, water everywhere
sometimes the air feels like rain

or a cobra coiling around oars
sucking them onto rocks
swirl of air, serpentine water
a divination of liquid death.
There is a pattern forming
the first cool wind rippling
goosebumps on your skin,
the rain tapping like a tattered man
with a stick
breaking into a wide roar
a certain prediction of storms.
The squat clouds burst
into a monsoon *raga*
a song to invoke Indra
demanding we understand water.
The storm prophets speak
of celestial signs–
the water calm
with stunned turtles
floating on waves
silent and awestruck
an awful silence
before a plaintive rumble
rising and falling–
the call of the sea.
The devil's voice
would stun Prospero
in his old palace
on winter nights
before his vanishing.
Day breaks a full hour
before its time
and all is seen in bright crimson
sails, men, sea, and clouds
a hemisphere of flame
the colour of cochineal
or dried blood.

Violent winds whirl
like giant Catherine wheels
knowledge collapses
in a whirlwind.
Space is filled with errant compass points
chaotic loops and spirals
classic preludes to the burst
from cloud bellies
ejaculated spume.
Far out at sea
even ships need new knowledge
how to read a storm
plot its course
and ride the crest like surfers.
The monsoon's roots
show in fishing nets muddy
with the muck of deep seas.
The storm thrashes up
things remembered from childhood
fairy tales told at night
under billowing nets
to ward off mosquitoes.
Once upon a time
Arabs mapped the seas with stories
unfurling accepted fictions
to find a route from one year to the next
without losing their way.
The first English on this coast
endured two monsoons
a short age for little gods
bent on empire.
They were the barrier
battered by sheets of water
vertical waves
slamming into their erect wills
washing away forbearance
like faces melting in the sea.

A bad time they had of it
no season for imperialists
used to controlling calm and catastrophe.
They'd dream
of divining thunder
reading Bengal light
as shipwreck signals
to illumine night
or Shiva's feet flashing fire.
No poetry, no consolation
no way to explain the cycle
where even an elephant god
dies at sea
no way to evade
the juggernaut
of torrential water
forcing all into the grip of tides
abandoning them like jetsam
from a million wrecks
submerged for deep-sea divers
to find and pin like old coins
to the rich felt of museums.
"No story quite resolved
not ending at the end"
this reborn season of submerged land.

AN IMPERFECT ARRANGEMENT

When I was growing up in Bombay, I made annual visits with my mother to the Catholic cemetery on All-Souls Day. Tombstones were my only contact with the ghost of my departed grandfather. Ewart Alimo died in his mid-fifties. I remember him only through family photographs and anecdotes by my mother. When I was born, his first grandchild, he frequented my parents' house simply to be allowed to carry me in his arms, up and down the long stone floor, dandling me, comforting me, uttering my name. The father of seven children, he obviously loved children, but he was cut short before he could enjoy a more expansive grandfatherhood. He is buried in sanctified ground, separated by thousands of miles from the resting places of Nellie Margaret, Valentine, Reginald, and Lorna. An imperfect arrangement for an apocalyptic resurrection.

There is a common family pattern for both sides of my parents. A familial disjunction, breakage, rifts. None of Ewart Alimo's grown children remained in Bombay; four went to England, one to Canada. And of the two left, Patricia and Edmund, there is little communication between them. Communiques are left for bereavements.

On my father's side, there is a nephew left in Bombay and a niece in England. And their children.

Immigration can be an act of distancing or alienation.

What were the Alimos trying to break away from? Simply a family discourse that could not see an admirable side? Simply the burden of cousins and aunts, uncles and step-father (the Englishman who had stayed on to marry their widowed mother)? Or was there a fear of inheriting the inexorable pattern of Anglo-India in exhaustion?

A fear of having come to the end of one's possibilities in that forbidding place.

ANGLO-INDIA

Anglo-India was less a concept or visionary place than merely something to be added to or subtracted from.

The Anglo-Indians of my acquaintance knew little of their own history and cared even less about it. Intellectually detached from such knowledge, they either despised or romanticized India's contradictions and their own ambivalent attitudes to these. The poor are always with us, they claimed piously, and the poor can teach us so much about humility of spirit and acceptance. But this sanctimony was false, no less than its opposite–contempt.

Some Anglo-Indians (and I knew several of these) still played polo, hunted wild boar, and hosted rowdy parties, but they, like their ancestors generations earlier, failed to make a true bridge between East and West, mistaking hospitality for true intimacy, preferring sport to philosophy. Few of them–only the best educated–knew anything about Indian gnosis. Many of them, pampered by unearned privilege, sought their own bourgeois El Dorado. At best, they were the epigones of Kipling or Scott; at worst, they were bastard progeny of imperial bastards.

Could I honestly set myself apart from all of them? I did not glorify Anglo-Indian life; but nor did I seek Indian philosophy. I did not attempt to reduce India to a formula; but nor did I try to understand her enigmas. I did not set myself apart from my Indian peers at school; but nor did I endeavour to become wholly a part of their communities.

Despite all too evident deficiencies culturally, morally, politically, Anglo-India was the side I joined with a half-guilty conscience by default of birth. At least Anglo-India had given me a language that was universally recognized, despite the exotic peculiarities of accent, rhythm, and diction. It was only away from Bombay that I became aware that words and phrases such as "*chota* peg," "bush-shirt," "mugging for exams," "Could you give me a lift?" or "box-*wallah*" did not have the sort of resonance to which I was accustomed.

My father spoke English but with a markedly different accent from mine, and with a syntax and diction that I found strange and often excruciating. Where others found his mangled phrases and malaprops amusing, I was embarrassed to hear him say "oinjment" instead of "ointment." When he declared of somebody "He suffers from magnesia" instead of "He suffers from amnesia," the gulf between us seemed unbridgeable.

"Where do you come from?" was a question I was too frequently asked after I arrived in Canada in 1961. I found it annoyingly patronizing because it assumed too many distinctions between myself and native-born Canadians. There were two ways I could have answered: one was by acknowledging that I was born in India; the other was by insisting on my bicultural ancestry. Both answers were somewhat embarrassing to me: the first because it carried an automatic freight of neo-colonialities; the second because it implicitly contained too much fiction.

To claim I was half-Armenian, without being able to speak or read a single Armenian word, would seem a prodigious exaggeration. On the other hand, to admit to being from India–however un-Indian I was in language, religion, custom, or sensibility–was tantamount to offering myself as an exotic "character," rather like the risible neo-colonial figures satirized by V.S. Naipaul.

There was an even more profound discomfort. I refused to allow my identity to be spread out so conveniently for a stranger's inspection. I was more complex than geography, more diverse than my passport suggested. My questioners were probably not attuned to my metaphysical disquiet. It was practically impossible for them to imagine that the differences in my parents' backgrounds were greater than anything ever established among whites in North America. It was a gross half-truth to be thought of as simply a product of intermarriage.

My father, a displaced Armenian, had reinvented himself as waiter and automobile mechanic in the Persian Gulf, and then as a respected executive of French Motors in Bombay. He was functionally literate–quite capable of dictating business reports and letters (which were polished by his secretary or my mother), but rage surpassed his linguistic ability. When he wrote, he was largely illegible, his script looking like spikey scratchings. He read newspapers but liked only those reports that massaged his own biases.

My mother was a colonial product but she was not in rebellion against her background. She seemed to have settled for middle-class comfort, resigned to the repeated rituals of Anglo-Indian life–the privileged indolence or ennui, assuaged by what Maud Diver called "promiscuous sociability" in the form of endless rounds of parties. She was not blind to my father's roughness, the near-calamitous state of his temper, but she thought of him as a diamond in the rough, and preferred to acknowledge his good qualities rather than his bad habits. She was not at all curious about his fragmented history or lost culture.

I was exogenous to Armenia, having grown up ignorant of my father's origins and language, and I was embarrassed at the wastefulness of much Anglo-Indian life. The very word "Anglo-Indian" had changed in significance. An Anglo-Indian used to mean someone of British descent who had settled in India, but the word gradually came to mean someone of mixed ancestry–someone half European and half Asian. There were surely Anglo-Indians of note in the British Raj, but in my Bombay adolescence, I could not find any contemporary Anglo-Indian of special significance. I went to a semi-private school which, like several others, had been originally built for Anglo-Indians and operated under the auspices of The Presidency Education Trust, but in my time there, the students of most exceptional note were Hindus and Parsis. Most of the Anglo-Indians I knew seemed to be adrift, either biding their time for some fervently imagined expatriation or resigned to being rejected by India and Britain.

There was no reflection of this tribe in Indo-Anglian writing, and certainly there was no Anglo-Indian attempt to portray this community to itself during my school years.

The Anglo-Indians of my generation were a dying breed, dying not only in terms of number but in cultural significance as well. The best they could hope for in the way of literary identity was in the novels of a vanished era by Rudyard Kipling, E.M. Forster, John Masters, and Paul Scott, and all these books were set in (real or fictive) places distant from Bombay. While it is true that the Anglo-Indians in Kipling are not the same as those in Forster or Masters or Scott, they all share a common fate as victims of Empire, for they are half-castes in a half-world of contempt, self-contempt, recrimination, evasion, and dispossession.

Of the four versions of life in Anglo-India, I found Kipling's the hardest to accept. It was filled with vulgar Cockney soldiers and their bawdy barrack ballads, *burra sahibs* and *memsahibs* who flourished in their clubs, and natives who were either patronized or brutalized. The English all played imperial roles that were totally incongruous to Indian poverty or acquiescence. Kipling's dialogue was tiresomely mannered, his characters and narrative voice usually representative of the ruling class that eventually left nothing but a shadow of itself in the Indian heat.

Forster and Scott were the most accurate writers on Anglo-India, but their fictional settings were of two different periods, Scott's Pankot postdating Forster's Edwardian Chandrapore by some twenty years. Moreover, Scott was more interested than Forster in charting the dying days of the Raj when the British (in his own words) "came to the end of themselves as they were." Scott saw India as being "even more than England was, the scene of the victory of liberal humanism over dying paternal imperialism." The special fascination that India had for Scott was "the almost tragic atmosphere" he saw as "attaching to it then" as "the mausoleum containing the remains of the last two great senses of public duty" the English had as a people: "the sense of duty that was part and parcel of having an empire, and the sense of duty so many [of the English] felt, that to get rid of it was the liberal human thing to do." Perhaps more than any other English novelist, Scott expressed in social terms the English ethos as a rigid attitude.

Forster, by contrast, was easily the most profound and imaginative interpreter of the philosophic tensions between the British and Indians. His English characters posed as gods in their assurance that Indians liked whatever deities were put in their path. Where Scott worked on an epical plane in *The Raj Quartet*, Forster managed to suggest a massive synthesis within a narrower frame in *A Passage To India*. Forster's novel brilliantly erects a synecdoche: the British Raj is a net cast over the subcontinent, but is itself entrapped by the insoluble mystery of what it seeks to control. When the English hear the enticing invitation, "Come," they are not really promised anything. The call is merely an appeal. And so the English come, seeking to take over and subjugate, but they remain invaders in exile. In fact, India catches them in her own massive "muddle." India's apparent formlessness overcomes them, for their imperial arrogance blinds them to the subtle pattern in a civilization "which the West can disturb but will never acquire."

Forster's great novel works magically by symbolism (cultural and metaphysical) and by assumptions about both England and India. It is a refined work of art that fans out from particular personal relationships into huge questions about race, philosophy, and psychic identity. The symbols of mosque, temple, and cave radiate centuries of history, theology, and metaphysics, but the English characters, apart from the good-hearted Mrs. Moore, are solidly rooted in nineteenth century values and assumptions about race and duty. They are bureaucrats, administrators, police officers, club men and women; they could form a partnership with the soldiers and officers in F. Yeats Brown's *Bengal Lancers*, a novel published six years after *A Passage To India*, but one that echoes Forster's quest for a synthesis of Indian dialectics through monism.

Less polished and subtle than Forster's novel, but raw and powerful in its own sensational way, John Masters' *Bhowani Junction* depicts an Anglo-India of a more recent period–the year prior to Indian independence, when nationalists were testing British moral and political willpower. A narrative in three voices–two Eurasian (Patrick Taylor's and Victoria Jones') and one English (Rodney Savage's)–*Bhowani Junction* expresses Anglo-Indian anxieties through a tale of sometimes savage lust and violence. The English despise the Anglo-Indians but need them, if only as visible consequences of Empire. The Anglo-Indians despise the Indians but need them, perhaps as a buffer between themselves and the English. Indian nationalism takes revenge on Anglo-Indians. The widow Sidarni Amrita Kasel, a patriot who has been jailed five times, articulates the Indian vengeance: "We're going to make you realize that you are Indians–inferior Indians, possibly disloyal Indians." Sneered at by the English and Indians, the Anglo-Indians are impelled to sneer at themselves. The emblem is a scorpion trying to kill itself.

The picture of the English holds no surprises: these colonials consolidate a class system to ensure imperialistic capitalism, and they are certainly not averse to inflicting any type of indignity as a form of political coercion. In one scene, Savage, the English lieutenant-colonel commanding a battalion of Gurkhas, orders his men to urinate on civil demonstrators lying across railway tracks. But the brutishness is not reserved for Indians alone; the Anglo-Indians, once considered "Domiciled Europeans," are branded "cheechees, half-castes, eight-annas, blacky-whites," and women such as Victoria Jones are considered fair objects for sexual violation. Rape, after all, can be an emblem of contempt and humiliation.

Colonialism breeds pigmentocracy, as the Anglo-Indians become almost pathologically colour-conscious. Mr. Jones, a senior driver on the Delhi Deccan Railway, and married to a dark-skinned wife who chews betel nuts in secret, encourages his daughter to lie about her background, suggesting that she claim to be partly Spanish in order to account for her swarthy complexion. And in a particularly bitter moment, Victoria recites a racial limerick to herself: "There was a young lady called Starkie/Who had an affair with a darkie./The result of her sins/Was an eightsome of twins–/Two black and two white and four khaki."

Victoria Jones sees the worst qualities of her tribe: "inferiority feelings, resentment, perpetual readiness to be insulted." Unable to be English because she is half-Indian, yet unable to be Indian because she is half-English, she is trapped by a double repudiation. Her people have no moral or political authority.

Bhowani Junction, which I first read as a link to the Technicolour M-G-M movie while I was a schoolboy, transcends its flaws as melodramatic or salacious literature because it contains sharp truths which compel Anglo-Indians to read themselves without self-pity. Its portrait of an Anglo-Indian railway cantonment is accurate, just as its racial and political dialectic is powerful.

The ending is a problem, though, because Victoria, physically glamorous, emotionally mature, ends up reconciling herself to her racial origins, despite all the preceding tensions that mitigate against such an ending.

But *Bhowani Junction*, on the whole, can be read with much profit. There are parallels between some of its characters and figures in my Bombay experience.

WATER OF MEMORY

Brilliant memoirist, especially of interior life, Annie Dillard has a writer's wisdom, and I love to soak in her writing. It is a sensory ecstasy, where my skin tingles as my eyes roam over her sentences. Yet I believe she may be wrong to claim that "when everything else has gone from [the] brain–the President's name, the state capitals, the neighborhoods where [one] lived, and then [one's] own name and what it was on earth [one] sought, and then at length the faces of [one's] friends, and finally the faces of [one's] family–when all this has dissolved, what will be left...is topology: the dreaming memory of land as it lay this way and that."

Topology and geography came to my writer's consciousness late, and they came more as metaphor and symbol than as literal data. It was only when I immersed myself in Canadian literature that I began to ponder such things as the lay of the land, the frontier experience, the far north, the true west, the garrison mentality, vertical man/horizontal world, the gothic wilderness.

As a child and, later, teenager in another country, I did not see my native city as a million points of light sprinkled and curved around a hillside and marina. Nor did I contemplate the thousand huts with dung fires burning in narrow, smokey doorways, or the neon glimmer of a multitude of apartments, the tall buildings lit in their pandemonium.

The topology has dissolved in large part from my memory, though I possess a dreaming memory of some of the lay of land.

–Malabar Hill suspended in rock and bower, manicured lawns, trellises, sculptured hanging gardens with hedges carefully shaped into animal forms, white villas with riotous bougainvillea, hibiscus, jasmine, and mulberry.

–-Marine Drive curving like a queen's necklace, and the taupe sands of Chowpatty, flecked with dark coconut shells bereft of their white inner flesh and "milk," abandoned plaintain leaves, cigarette wrappers, pebbles unclaimed by the tow of tide, and the remains of fish, spiny, mottled, urned in shell or tattooed by bird beak.

Having been born near water, I have read water. Shallow and deep, limpid, scummy, foamy, amniotic, saline, subversive, tempestuous, placid, psychic. Taken the waters. Tested them. Mixed water and powders. Milk and water. Scotch and water. Stepped into the same river twice, but never the same water. Stirred, like Raphael, the water of memory. Gazed, like Narcissus, at mirror water.

Water inspires nostalgia and desire–both forms of death. We sometimes yearn for what has already passed, and what we desire are only ghosts of presences. Desire evaporates as it is born.

I am a travelling swimmer, though no Ned Merrill. Nude skin as a metaphor of life, survival: in waters that are charted, measurable, and usually safe. Water is friction too, as is the body resisting both it and air, pushing itself over (invisible) acqueous planes.

Swimming is also geometry by composition. Arrangement of strokes, limnable limbs, unadorned, unalloyed, angles and arcs.

But swimming is symbology. The water embraces you, desires foreplay. Dares you to reveal more skin, even your blemishes and carnal imperfections. It wants your body in its passionate flux. It refuses to let you manhandle it.

It refuses to be contained, restrained, chained. It invents its own rules, inverts rules, and it is never one-dimensional. It is delusory. It is water of difference, deferring its mystery, sometimes even its power.

I am often up to my neck in it.

I wish to inscribe my body on it. Learn to write on water.

Water is woman. It drinks Ophelia. It consumes Narcissus. Prospero's books drown in water.

Bombay rose gently above sea level, but the greatest density of life was on low-lying planes, where a sea of people billowed over with the passions of everyday life. The city was so congested that no stray dog, its bones almost poking through paper-thin skin, could ever run the length of a street without bumping into a person. Oaks and banyans, palm trees and fig trees grew in abundance, and fruit and flower preened in their green surroundings, the people entangled among one another in humid exhaustion while ceiling fans and hand *punkahs* whirred and fluttered.

Nothing could shut out the sun–not the sway-backed palms, the hirsute banyans clumped like aged orangoutangs, the intermittent sharp-thorned mulberry bushes, the fig trees raided by song birds discarding pitted fruit skins, or the guava trees smelling of hard green fruit. The birds twittered, whistled, shrieked, and ruffled the leaves, vibrating the leaner boughs with whirring feathers and choreographed feet.

At high noon, everything was a blurred shimmer as the city appeared to vapourize. Dogs panted with exhaustion, beggars shielded their filmy eyes from the unforgiving sun, urchins gathered around shop hoses spraying short bursts of cold water–charity from merchants. Bombay still had victorias in the fifties, and as patrons travelled incognito behind the black window flaps, the lean horses laboured uphill and down, slipping on the hot asphalt, wheezing with the effort of being beasts of burden, as the carriage-drivers flicked their long whips at the animals, now foaming at the bits between their teeth. Occasionally a horse would drop to its knees and then feel the lash on its scarred flanks.

The unforgiving heat exacerbated the stench of dung. "Indians defecate everywhere," wrote V.S. Naipaul in *An Area of Darkness*, pointing to the streets, beaches, hills, and river banks polluted by squatters who were for the longest time deliberately omitted from novels or stories, feature films or documentaries. Canine, feline, bovine, equine, human excrement–all mingled in what Salman Rushdie called "a brotherhood of shit" in *Midnight's Children*. And it is true, the excremental vision was ineradicable.

As was the spectacle of beggary. Bombay had a multitude of poor: legless, ragged grotesques wheeling themselves on their versions of skate-boards which they pushed with scrawny hands, blistered and scraped raw with the effort; blind children with dark flies gathering around their gummy sockets; lepers with suppurating sores; victims of elephantiasis, swollen horrors who lumbered along with tumid legs or arms. These indigents besieged everyone, everywhere. I find it difficult to write of them, nearly four decades after witnessing their perpetual horror.

Their spectacle was always an expression of Indian stasis. In Bombay, poverty was part of an Indian design of acquiescence to fate, but some of the poor tried turning their deprivation into theatre. There was a fairly young man who used to limp into The Retreat to sing for alms. Sensing that English could be useful in this context, he would deliver in a rather hoarse, off-key voice "Daisy, daisy, give me your answer doo," or "You are my sun-sine, my only sun-sine." The lyrics were always punctuated by resounding slaps to his own bare stomach, as if to dramatize the hollow in its pit. "You are my sun-sine," [slap] "my only sun-sine," [slap] "You make me happee," [slap] "when skies are gray." [slap]

It was necessary, then, to force aside these images and wish for fresh ice-cold lemonade on the verandah or the beach in the morning or even the rock pools of the hills.

FEET: A META-GEOGRAPHY

As the family photographs fade, I harbour other memories... traces of what my parents left in my consciousness. Such as the talcum powder my father used on his feet after bathing, the cigarette burns on wooden furniture, the rings left on tables from his drinking glasses. The smell of my mother's shampooed hair, the Cutex for her fingernails, the silhouettes of the dresses in her closet.

And always the colour, shape, texture, and smell of skin.

My mother, a petite woman barely five feet tall, had smooth, unblemished, creamy soft skin. Her delicate fingers weren't strong enough to open jars or bottles, and her tiny, well-shaped feet could have slipped easily into the glass slipper of fairy-tale fame. I could always smell the scent of Pears soap on her, and though she was no Gibson girl, she could seem especially attractive when powdered, rouged, and lipsticked. "Every son thinks his mother is beautiful, I guess–and to every son, every mother is beautiful in ways that have nothing to do with features, nothing to do with graces–everything to do with tones of voices, assurances, the touch of finger ends." (Timothy Findley, *The Piano Man's Daughter*)

My father was short, a mere five feet four, stocky, and raw. He had pink skin, and his well-muscled arms and legs had power that I admired. He had little body hair and no discernible nicks, bumps, ridges, or depressions in his skin. His fingers and toes were chunky and hard, quite incapable of grace but assuredly suited to quotidian chores. I studied the way he used to wash his oil-stained hands at lunchtime when he returned from the garage. The soap used to bubble brown or black with the grease, and no matter how briskly he would rub his fingers and palms together, there was always a residue of grime under his fingernails, an unexpunged sign of his preoccupation with machines. His feet had a heavy tread, and I could hear his footfall but not my mother's. Sometimes after work, when his socks were off, his feet smelled like Gorgonzola.

Feet had their own geography for me. Ankles could be jutting abutments, heels could be curving ridges, soles soft valleys, and the slope from the lower shin to the toes could have an aesthetic sign. But toes held me by their mystery. Unsheathed, they could leave their imprint on the smooth tiled floors. As a toddler, when my mother and her neighbourhood women friends sat down to afternoon bridge and rummy, I would crawl under a table and watch their feet which, inevitably, slipped out of slipper or shoe to rest nakedly before my curious eyes.

Feet told me something about their owners, though my articulations were developed much later. There were some that did nothing other than rest flat on the floor. These, I imagined, belonged to the women who were satisfied with dull conformity. They were incapable of skipping or dancing lyricism. They expected nothing beyond an hour or more of sedentary passivity. There were other feet that were sometimes restless, as they rubbed against one another in a sort of nervous dance. They belonged, perhaps, to women who were timid at home, subject to their husbands and not quite certain of where they wanted to move in life. Then there were feet where toes wiggled or squirmed, and sometimes curled in an attempt to be sinuous. Perhaps they belonged to women who were capable of vanity, capable of excited pleasure.

I used to study my own skin and the shape of my toes. I was relieved not to find any dry scales like those the women sometimes scraped off their older feet. My curiosity was not restricted to this serious self-examination. As the ladies were deep into their idle gossip and calculated bidding, I would decide which feet had the greatest interest for me, and then take as big a bite as I could manage of the enticing toes.

A sudden cry would interrupt the cardgame. "What was that?" someone would inquire. "That damn child just bit my toes!"

To this day, I am carnally drawn to attractive feet, though I draw the line at sipping champagne out of a lady's slipper, however silken or perfumed.

This is my meta-geography, a sensual imprint that is probably a variant of my father's sensual interest in some other part of human anatomy.

JESUITS, SHRI, AND SEX

Like some of D.H. Lawrence's characters, I had sex on the brain as an adolescent. Attendance at an exclusively boys' school did not help. Denied female peers, we were left to our own devices about our hormonal urges, and although I loved to burrow in an infinitude of books in my quieter moments, I could not deny tumescence.

Because we all had sisters, aunts, and female neighbours, we did not regard the opposite sex as creatures of absolute mystery. However, denied the bewildering social truth of their company, we looked on girls as a conspiracy created against us by paranoid elders. There were no dances at our school, and our socials were the most pristinely homosexual imaginable, given the overwhelming maleness, though entirely lacking in sex except in the mind. They were bizarre affairs, chaperoned by teachers and asexual parents.

St. Mary's had too many Jesuits to be anything other than muffled about sex and growing boys. We envied the Protestants who attended co-ed Christ Church where, we fantasized, the student population could meet, hold hands, and negotiate however furtively the first transactions of young lust. What were their dances like? Where did the boys put their warm hands? How did they camouflage spontaneous erections? Did the girls and boys address one another by witty names embedded with sexual codes? At St. Mary's we had to be content with slandering teachers ("Big Bum," "Charlotte the Harlot," *et cetera*) or with insulting one another's parents. Socialization took clumsy forms: we slapped one another on shoulders and backs, arm-wrestled vigorously, ridiculed shy peers by vaudevillian mimickry, and exaggerated our own untested sexual prowess by complicit winks and lies. We wished ourselves to be walking gods, but often revealed ourselves as comical beasts.

We were lectured relentlessly about self-control, but in sexual terms, we failed to develop any selves worth controlling. The lives of girls and women were meant to be of no concern to us, of even less significance than the sexual lives of nuns and priests which, ironically, became springboards for our lewdest fantasies and gossip. Denied sex, we had to invent it with our imaginations.

We took little comfort in our priests' assurances that there would be something grand ahead for us. Virginity was to be prized, they said. Whatever we needed in order to meet the future was to be found in the classroom, gymnasium, or on the playing field. Most of us remained sceptical. Where the boys of Christ Church had dances and socials as carnal outlets, we had to be celibate and amuse ourselves with volleyball, soccer, and cricket. The boys of Christ Church were given a headstart at becoming informed about the real world, while most of us weren't even given dancing lessons, not having anyone except our mothers to dance with.

At home, I did learn the elementary box-step but was too shy to elaborate on it, and I suspect that even if a seriously carnal girl had come my way, I would not have known how to handle the situation. The closest I ever came to teenage sex was at a party when a dark-skinned beauty in a tight-fitting red dress sat beside me and exercised her full repertoire of flirtation. Noticing my interest in her almost sheath-like dress, she coaxed me into touching the fabric directly at her knee. I blushed, and the adults in the room enjoyed my discomfort. The result for me was stupefying paralysis.

Classes at St. Mary's ran from Monday to Saturday, with a midweek break on Thursday. Christ Church and Clare Road Convent School had breaks on Saturday, so there seemed to be yet another conspiracy against us by the Jesuits, who forced us into minor self-mortification by their cycles of benedictions, sermons, confessions, and retreats, all very pointedly aimed at getting us to move away from private parts to the saints. Outside of masturbation, the only ejaculations we had were the phrases uttered during church litanies.

Spiritually descended from both St. Ignatius Loyola and Torquemada, the Jesuits turned sex into a demonic force. It was sinful to even have thoughts about sex, let alone perform it. They lined us up for weekly confession during Lent, and our confessors demanded an exact accounting of our impure thoughts, words, and deeds. And at the annual retreat, one pink-faced priest in black cassock conducted a highly theatrical presentation on the Last Judgement. A coffin draped in black to the left of the communion rail, he sat at a long table on the right, scribbling pensively in an imposing black ledger as two candles flickered ominously. The penumbral setting heightened the morbidity, and the only thing that precluded terror was our knowledge of this priest's genial eccentricity outside the holy of holies. He often wandered absent-mindedly about the schoolyard in his curry-stained white soutane, and his footwear alternated between sneakers with large holes at the toe or scuffed leather shoes which he would scratch whenever an itch beset him. Consequently, it was impossible to accept him in the role of God decreeing eternal damnation.

Our parents maintained a firm silence on all things sexual. They were still suffering from residual Victorianism which decreed an injunction on sex education. It wasn't simply one kind of love that dared not speak its name. Consequently, young boys received their information from older chums. I saw my first "pornographic" image at twelve. It was an explicit black and white postcard of a Parisian whore and her "john," and I remember the look of amazement on her face as she handled his gigantic erection.

Strange the injunctions against sex in a country where peasant women breastfed their babies openly on buses, trams, and trains, and where *coolies* walked around naked, except for their loin cloths which barely concealed phalluses sometimes dangling like slender aubergines. Stranger still the injunctions in a country which was saturated with sexual symbolism and ritual. Indians worshipped the *yoni* and the *lingam*. When passing a sculpture of the Goddess Shri, it was customary for a Hindu to touch her sacred mound, the *yoni*. South Indian temples had a sculpture of two holy men in prayer beneath a giant-sized vulva. Shri Lakshmi, the goddess of abundance, held one hand to a breast (source of milk and nurture) while her other hand pointed to her vulva, the sacred threshold of birth.

There is also evidence that members of a certain Vishnu sect paint on their foreheads an emblem of the ripe vulva of a menstruous woman. And the lotus is a sexual emblem in India, its bloom a symbol of women's labia, its bud a symbol of a virgin vagina, and its pistil a representation of the foetus. Thus, the entire flower is meant to suggest the womb.

Ancient caves had the most amazing erotic carvings with sexual positions that would be the envy of most sex manuals. Nudity was not fig-leafed or veiled. The Hindus believe that every nude woman incarnates *prakrti*, nature, matter, the primordial substance. She is the prototype of woman. Without her *shakti* or primal energy, the male, human or god, is dormant or lifeless.

Looking back on my adolescence, I am still confounded by adult reticence about sex.

I am especially confounded by my father's silence. In any conflict between mind and body, the body would win in my father's case. A lusty man, he could never seem to keep his hands off my mother on the verandah after dinner, massaging her breasts gently, without any evident concern that his children might be watching.

THE CONSEQUENCES OF WORDS

When I entered high school, I became increasingly aware that my parents' reading would never go to *my* head. My father read only the daily newspaper, auto magazines and technical guides, and the occasional popular biography. He was not a simpleton. It is simply that intellectualism was *terra incognita* to him. My mother, a more cultivated individual, seemed to wither in her literary taste, moving from the classics to modern romances and scandal magazines. Most of the books at home were mine.

I started collecting them in a stout, wooden, blue-gray trunk, circa British India army, stencilled with the name and rank of my godfather, Charles Ronald Williams, a large man with an overwhelmingly jolly disposition but a core of deep sadness. A bachelor all his life who had been jilted several times, he was Falstaffian in humour, teaching me inadvertently that every comic has a potentially tragic underside. The life of any party, he would regale us all with vividly droll anecdotes and mimicry before succumbing to a maudlin melancholy from whose center he would sing sad Portuguese love songs.

He, too, alas, was no reader to any significant degree. So, I went about my fascination with books, beginning perhaps with a sensory lust in the smell of glossy jackets, the exotic creamy paper of hardbacks, with elegantly stitched binding around gilt-edged pages that could be fluttered like a surprised covey of birds.

I loved the Penguin classics in their cream and orange covers. As for poetry, I dipped into Oscar Williams' *Great Poems of the English Language* and, of course, Palgrave's *Golden Treasury*, the latter being literally a pocket-book, nine centimetres by fourteen and a half, with a range of lyrics "by writers not living–and none beside the best." I had a passing familiarity with Shelley, Keats, and Wordsworth, Sir Walter Scott, Emerson, Kipling, Swinburne, Arnold, Browning, and Tennyson long before I ever learned to read them seriously and in depth at university. When my hormones began to rage and sexual fantasy preoccupied my idle hours, I could turn to the prose of the *Kama Sutra* or *The Perfumed Garden* or *The Pillow Book* before seeking the poetic ravishment of Edward Fitzgerald's translation of Omar Khayyam, though not in Palgrave's staid volume. Many a tumid hour was spent in the company of the paperback edition published by Jaico Publishing House, replete with provocative line-drawings by Gordon Ross, particularly of naked or semi-naked women bending over delightful herbs and tender greens or nestling in a lover's arms where "with a loaf of bread beneath the bough,/A flask of wine, a book of verse–and Thou" they and I turned wilderness into "Paradise enow." My chum Alan Oscar once vanished into his washroom with a copy of the unexpurgated *Rubaiyat* and didn't emerge for a considerable time, though when he did, his face was flushed as a sly smile crept over it.

As a Catholic, I was later fed a diet of exemplary hagiographic biographies, *Lives of the Saints* with their graphic martyrdoms which could well have been instances of soft-core pornography, especially when I recall the iconic illustrations of a lamb-bearing Saint Agnes with her virginal throat offered to the pervert's knife or of Saint Sebastian looking for all the world like a particularly handsome bodybuilder in a loin-cloth, albeit pierced with phallic arrows. (No wonder artists such as Pasolini and Jarman and Mishima have used Saint Sebastian in their varied discourses on human desire.)

Religion–or, perhaps, religiosity–accounted for some of my early reading material: Cardinal Spellman's novel, *The Foundling*, Fulton Sheen's genial, optimistic sermons, Fulton Oursler (I can't remember what or why), Thomas à Kempis, Frank Sheed, Hillaire Belloc, G.K. Chesterton's *Orthodoxy* (far too sophisticated in its epigrams and paradoxes for my juvenile mind), Tom Dooley (the doctor-missionary and not the subject of ballad fame), and Ronald Knox. Though Catholicism burned guilt into my soul, I tried to be catholic in my reading. I mixed Protestant, Jewish, Hindu, and Taoist material with my staunchly Catholic syllabus.

My eclectic reading turned me into a mimic writer, someone who was adept at imitating the contours of various writers' crafts without being able to invent his own. Perhaps, however, such mimicry had a great virtue: it made me appreciate the value and range of writing, even critical writing, as a high definition performance, just as with acting, bullfighting, singing, cricket, et cetera. It is possible to find a different voice for a different purpose.

Which returns me to the question of mimicry, an inveterate theme of Anglo-India where the mimicry changed with fashion faster than the inner world did. There were the English place-names: Breach Candy (a swimming pool in the actual shape of India reserved for Europeans only), Brabourne Stadium (where I took in my first Australia versus India cricket test match, after playing truant from school), Willingdon Club, Warden Road, Kemp's Corner, Queen's Court, Annie Besant Road, Flora Fountain, Ballard Pier, Cadell Road, Elphinstone College, Prince of Wales Museum. There were the queer nicknames, often applied to non-Anglo-Indians: Bunty, Sonny, Queenie, Jumbo, Jiggs, and Piggy (the last metamorphosed into Piggins for a lady). There were the school-ties and blazers, a legacy of English prep schools. There were the English *Boys' Own* annuals, English films (everything from classical adaptations, mysteries and romances to costume dramas, and bawdy farces, and with stars from Olivier and Leigh, to Donat and Garson, from Lockwood and Mason to Joyce Grenfell and Alistair Sim), and English music (orchestras and bands were very much the rage in Bombay, though the trend to Indianization was growing). There were the exotic culinary concoctions, beverages, and desserts: kedgeree, cutlets, sardines on toast, cottage bread, Pimm's Cup, suet pudding, Spotted Dick, trifle –"the food of exiles," as Forster noted, "[made] by servants who did not understand it." There were the prescribed Cambridge reading lists: from Shakespeare, Dickens, and Stevenson to *Lays of Ancient Rome*, *Midlothian*, and *Trent's Last Case*. Nothing, of course, by Narayan, Malgonkar, Raja Rao, Mulk Raj Anand, Ruth Prawer Jhabvala. These were writers I discovered in Canada as a resident alien.

And yet I was not of England. I knew that as surely as I knew that it was not ridiculous to read of Dickens' wintry London or Wordsworth's daffodils or Shelley's skylark. Nor was it ridiculous to sing "When Irish Eyes Are Smiling," "Danny Boy," or "Auld Lang Syne." We were all colonized, we recognized this as such, and felt we were the better for it. There were worlds elsewhere, to which we were not denied entry.

I had simply not yet found my place.

From my reading shall you know me, for reading was a way for me to find my place. I claim books as reader and writer. Their creators are sometimes my *alter ego*. I am their salacious mirror, a crypto-critic intent on doubling my pleasure by usurping their language (chronically) and (less frequently) their ideas.

I want fiction, friction, crypto-friction. I want stories that show us how they became stories. I want to make love to imagination, whatever the accidents of my birth and upbringing.

My reading is homage that hones the consequences of words.

And I write also as homage to words. This book is composed of personal journeys made in the shadow of elegy, and while my obvious vehicles are memories (particularly memories of wounds), my fuel is forms of language I hold most dear to my being.

I pay homage in a minor key to a triumph of the ephemeral.

SIMPLY THE THING I AM

Books redeemed the silence between myself and my father. I looked to them for the wisdom I believed he lacked, for the language beyond his understanding, for the sheer sensuousness of paper, design, typography, illustration–the very things to which he was indifferent–and, as such, books became my textual father. I could go to them for discourses outside his ken or sympathy. They showed me universes denied to him. I could enter into a mental dialogue with them, and dialogue was one thing truly absent in my relationship with my father. We might as well have been from different planets. I wanted a world that was palpably different from his.

My father was a king in his profession. His clients had full faith in his expertise and trusted his business integrity. In his workshop he thundered orders over the din of machinery and he was lord of the domain, with mechanics fairly bowing and scraping before him so that they would not be "given hell." But I felt that he was more dedicated to his work than he was to the task of being a father to his son.

Albert Camus wrote: "A man's work is nothing more than to rediscover, through the detours of art, those one or two images in the presence of which his heart first opened." Automobile mechanics was my father's "art," but what did such greasy, soiled work generate in the way of soul-enlarging imagery? Perhaps, his work was no more than a way of creating a "ritual space," a different place for what brought him satisfaction, status, and generous gifts from grateful clients. It was common for him to bring home large baskets of oranges or melons or mangoes, bottles of Scotch or *crême de menthe*. His children's birthdays were celebrated with parties at which there was an ice-cream cake courtesy of Joy Ice-Cream, whose owner had learned his business in the States and was one of my father's prestigious customers. And every New Year's Eve, we would be given an entire suckling pig, roasted to perfection, with apple in mouth, and paper-thin skin crackling with salty savour, the meat beneath tender and sweet.

His work was a golden feather of a firebird, but it was only a single feather, and he never did win the whole creature.

I was secretly proud of his professional achievement, though I stubbornly sought to move in a line directly away from it. I was incompetent in the handling of machines and quite content to remain so. I noted his power, rough temper, and competitiveness, and knew that these strong qualities were also in some way the source of his independence, courage, technical skill, and uprightness. His colleagues and clients respected him highly, even though some of his staff found his brusque fortrightness abrasive.

He was quick to find fault and he strained at the bit to pick quarrels. He was not easily moved to forgive or forget a slight or indignity. There was a cruel streak in his kingship, and from an early age, I rejected him as one not worthy of my reverence.

Although I knew that his success was heroic, having been achieved after the almost unbearable pain of his Armenian history, I considered him a bully who revelled in his power to impress others, proclaim his superiority, and assert his right to dominate those around him. And he was impatient. This warrior might stab the firebird through the heart, simply to have one more golden feather.

I resented him for filling the home with his shadow.

He was not my hero or my king. I transferred my hero-worship and fealty to other royalty: Shakespeare and Laurence Olivier.

Of course, we clashed because of our contrary natures and temperaments, and when we did, I sometimes became histrionic in my anger, prompting him to ask acidly: "And who are you playing today? You're not Olivier, you know."

My father was a Spencer Tracy fan because he liked the actor's scale, sincerity, and photographic realism. Tracy never seemed to raise his voice. My father considered Olivier too florid and loud. "He shouts too much," he complained, missing the rich textures in his voice. Naturally, we were diametrically opposed on this, as on any other subject. Quite apart from his wittily romantic, erotic, and heroic acting that incorporated a thrilling vocal technique, physical poise, fluency of movement, and interpretive imagery that was sometimes surrealistic rather than merely realistic, Olivier represented the sort of male figure I wanted to be. He was the hero with whom I identified through my adolescence and youth. I knew he was the *non pareil* of actors, but I felt instinctively from his film performances (I was to see him on stage only three times in Montreal in 1967 when he led a company in plays by Strindberg, Congreve, and Feydeau) that he was my "spiritual" model. In my secret self, I was witty, romantic, and erotic. Like his offstage self,

I was imprinted with a solitary essence or a shy self-protectiveness that sometimes needed to be cunningly crafted. Like him (with his wives and adoring fans) I could not entrust my life to anyone. I was unwilling to be taken over–a stubbornness that has often brought me grief in personal and professional relationships, without necessarily diminishing my belief that, perhaps, pain validates conviction. When I am confident about an idea or concept, I dig in my heels defiantly and exude the passionate energy of one who dares to invite anarchy.

I am simply the thing I am.

SECOND COUNTRY

My parents decided jointly to immigrate to Canada in 1961. They knew little of the country, except what was reported by family friends, the Kulhanians, and their long-widowed Indian mother who had first gone to England and then, more wisely, to Canada. The United States had been our expatriate friends' original choice, but entry was virtually impossible at the time, even with American cousins willing to offer sponsorship. England had been the second choice, and Canada, perhaps because of its proximity to the States, their third.

My parents decided on Canada by a process of elimination. England, the putative Home for displaced or disgruntled Anglo-Indians, would have been my mother's logical choice, especially as her elder sister, younger brothers, and mother had already selected their respective homesites there, ranging from Birmingham to Stoke-on-Trent and London. Two nephews and a niece of my father were also in England, two in London and one in Middlesex. But my mother recoiled from the reality of English damp and cold. Canada, of course, was even colder, but central heating was not alien to it or deemed an expensive luxury. My mother could not see herself warming up her English bed with hot-water bottles and layers of thick blankets after feeding innumerable shillings to a gas meter. Nor did she fancy English soot or chilly English reserve.

My father, having been sent from Bombay on business-training to Sheffield and Nuffield, had, by contrast, a more sentimental view of England. To him it was a country of quaint cottages and inns, the easy chatter and choral singing at the local pub, the conscientious cleanliness of gloved vendors, the proper manners of the English gentleman.

Like all other Armenians in Bombay, he insisted on being classified with Europeans. He claimed, as did many other Armenians, that his people belonged to the Aryan race, which divided itself into three main branches: the Nordic, the Alpine, and the Mediterranean. As some historians pointed out, Armenians belonged to a family of the Alpine branch, whose original source was Central Europe. The Armenian language belonged to the Germanic group of Indo-European languages.

My father believed that all the rights and privileges conferred on the Armenians in India by the East India Company Charter or Agreement of 1688, and since maintained, guaranteed not only the protection of Armenian churches, educational and charitable foundations, or landed properties and commerce, but the important status of British Indian subjects with just claims to be classified with Europeans.

So, England was my father's first choice because he felt specially protected by the English. Both my parents knew the facts of English racism–the revenge of defeated imperialists who had no more glory. Reluctantly, my father abandoned the idea of England as a new home.

Australia skimmed across my parents' minds as an option. The climate would be more congenial than England's, and there were long beaches and sparkling warm waters where one could be in one's proper element, despite reconnoitring sharks. But Australia also had vile defects: it fancied itself a supremely masculine culture where women were "Sheilas," and might as well have been drovers' cattle; its class barriers were probably as repulsive as England's; and, even before I ever read Patrick White, Australia did not seem to transcend its dichotomy as a garden-desert.

So Canada was chosen. Or chose us.

We had to apply to the Canadian consulate, give assurances (with references and evidence) that we were solvent, of good character, sound health and citizenship. What was our purpose for seeking landed immigrant status? India held no future for his children, my father maintained. Canada held infinitely more possibilities.

The truth was I never felt at one with Bombay. I yearned for a different country, though not necessarily with snow, *portages*, *coureurs de bois*, and quaint cedar cabins secluded in a bear-dark wood near a lake of loons. Canada came to me in disjointed images and stereotypes. I knew, of course, of the Royal Canadian Mounted Police. Didn't they always get their man? But what did this mean? Canada was a country of resettled felons, like Australia? On the other hand, there were Diefenbaker and Pearson, hardly emblematic of hewers of wood and drawers of water. One had wavy silver hair, the jowls and teeth of a chipmunk, and the eyes of an owl; the other had an absurd polka-dot bowtie, a cowlick, and an interesting lisp. They were both extremely conservative, decent, and safe. Not at all the sort who would send out U-2's or threaten the use of intercontinental ballistic missiles, like the Americans; not the sort who would divide and rule a nation like the British had done.

We could entrust ourselves to their governance.

After the obligatory interview with a Canadian attaché–in which my mother exaggerated my proficiency in oral French–and after manipulating our way out of the muddle of Indian bureaucracy, with our pecuniary duty discharged to the peon who told us that "Pirst we must have pee" (meaning "fee"), and, in another venue, after dutifully discharging our urine into neatly labelled bottles in Dr. Callander's office, we were stamped, classified, innoculated, and decreed fit for passage on board H.M.S. *Arcadia*.

Our vessel portended utopia, although we knew that the connotation was a volitional act of imagination.

My two younger sisters and I were exultant with expectation. My father resigned himself to a social and financial decline in fortunes. My mother was dewy-eyed at the farewell party when friends joined hands in a large ring and sang "Auld Lang Syne."

We donated furniture and china, gold ornaments and odds-and-ends of our Bombay home to my cousin, Neville, and were careless about what we tried to dispossess. My passion for collecting was ruthlessly limited to a couple of hundred books, school yearbooks, and assorted papers and clippings having to do with painting, literature, film, and theatre. We were almost obscene in our haste to strip down the volume of our baggage. I wanted India to fall away like dead skin.

The single tragic note was the death of the family pet, our beautiful black and white Alsatian, Lassie, a mere three and a half years old, who leaped off a friend's balcony to go desperately in search of us the day we placed her in her adoptive home. As crates and suitcases formed stalagmites in our house, Lassie sensed that something traumatic was about to befall her. She was panic-stricken after leaping off the second-floor balcony, and confused and disoriented, she wandered directly into the path of a double-decker bus.

We were *en route* to London from Southampton when news reached us of her death, and I was grief-stricken with guilt. Life was a sequence of betrayals, but why did I have to be implicated?

I irritated some family friends on the day of our May departure by complaining that Bombay was too hot, too humid. They felt I was being too colonial, that I was assuming the pose of a tourist who did not find the place worthy of his interest. Perhaps there was an alternative version: I was being prematurely an agent of self-transformation, wishing eagerly to be displaced and remade.

Arriving in Montreal in June, 1961, a month before my eighteenth birthday, was the beginning of a new history, even a new language. I expressed the feeling in a poem, "The Second Language," published in *Impulse* in the Fall of 1973.

In the morning we sail up the river
Looking at the glassy water
Pale green, too cold for life.
On the banks are grey fires
Wisping into the sun
and expiring in heaven.
The Nova Scotian on deck
Is dressed in tweed
And smokes a pipe,
Smiles, and in his Atlantic tone
Tells us that his province
Is far warmer than Quebec.
I think he means the people.
At sea it is hard to know
Where only suspirations can be felt
While the realities lie on shore.
In the afternoon the Nova Scotian says
That we are reaching Montreal
Because there is a rumour of a foreign tongue,
A large suggestion of an alien language.
He assures us that the people are not all bad
But "There are two solitudes, you know."
No more at sea
I prepare to become part
Of a foreign vocabulary.
When I walk ashore
The land retracts
Like an evil slander
Which I survive.
The customs official whispers
Words without subtitles
While I root about for missing papers
To be validated in two languages
With accents quite different from my own.

Four years later came another poem about the same subject. "Second Country" was published in *Echo*.

I

Amid new explorers
making fresh surveys
scanning the ice-ribbed country
frozen congealing
I wait

Not altogether one of them
scanning too
but thinking differently.
My mind drips images
of a house I left.

II

The first house fading,
I breathe
in the still, ice air
which locks me
in a different climate.

III

Remembering now
that first country,
burning in hot sun
like dry crust too hard to nourish.

I do not have to portage
across this white map
with names like sounds of drums
beating about my head
reeling a history of the dispossessed.
A people owned this map
before it was coloured white.
Can I melt the ice
around its edges

and change the legend?

IV

Someone called:
The foreigner!
Or was it just water whispering to shore
breaking through ice,
frozen suspicion, dotted by *habitants*
with white eyes
dry, mono toned
like waste paper and powdered snow
blowing together.

V

I am here
on this white map   discoloured
by images dripping
out of memory.
But whispers still come
out of the cracking ice and peeling shore
behind the white eyes staring neurally
and the taut throats swallowing suspicion
of my language.

VI

This land is a picture
I hold in eye
unmoving water in a glass
reflecting in white light
all the ice   the shipless water.

I now know that the two poems are a curious struggle between text and life. Already, then, unbeknownst to me, I was preparing to write this memoir, with one theme being the profound act of displacement.

I was adaptable but alien, willing, it seems, to hint at a story under the surface. The covert story of what I might have been if we had not left Bombay.

Does the absent story matter? Is it simply a road not taken, a crypto-fiction in friction with my self and its mirror-image?

The covert story under the snow and ice, is not of Canadian reticence or of volitional dispossession and appropriation; it is a refusal to deal with the undesired past.

PART TWO

Armenia

ELEGY

Saturday, November 25,1995

Vile wind in winter wetness
driving through the ice tremble
and the bone-dust ghost-forsaken
sinks into watery relic.

He died, we were told, in his sleep, unable to reach for water on the table, unable to gasp out his plague of thirst. His mouth was a black hole, caught with grotesque suddenness in the *rigor mortis* of unspoken havoc.

It was a moment I had long anticipated, dreaded, and desired.

A wild man had shrunk incontestably into the final truth of mortality.

My sister and I embraced in grief but I could not weep. Some other force was taking over, as if there were some ineffable release, some long-expected collapse of tensions, leaving me free and yet in some sense unprepared.

I noted how small his emaciated body seemed, as if the bones and shrivelled skin were the relics of an ultimate abandonment. Some vast beyond had swallowed his spirit, and gone were the terrible ferocity of his bitter anger, the huge appetite for sensual indulgence, the protracted agony of filling in stretches of empty old age with the habits of decrepitude and an unspoken but undeniable longing to reject death.

I prayed for the repose of his soul, I prayed that the ancient bad feelings between us would die out. Had I known the Armenian word then, I would have wished him benevolent *hankisd*... rest. Rest.

My father had often spoken about the miseries of old age, yet when death seemed closest, he had never spoken about last things. Even as he rasped through dry, burning lips, he wanted to face one more round of tortuous dependency on the kindness of others.

"I'm grateful," he had barely whispered when two family friends, the Kulhanian sisters, had made a long trek from Vancouver to console him.

It was a peculiar time. My father and I had long been spiritual adversaries–he, unable to understand my nature and sensitivities; I, unwilling to permit my sympathy for his boyhood nightmares to prevail against my anger at his wild power.

Perhaps neither of us had been capable of facing ourselves.

He had not wanted to die. He had liked staying alive, despite his enormous infirmities. But what was he afraid of meeting in death? The souls of all his murdered kin? The spectres of his deceased daughter and docile wife? Or my unvoiced accusations of his indiscriminate violence of will and action?

DZOUR

Armenians are defined by their argumentativeness. My father's conversations at parties and around the family table invariably led to disagreements, often at the top of his voice, about anything from religion, politics, and technology to literature, movies, and social customs. Perhaps because he was so vilely deprived of a formal education, he wanted to assert himself–to show that he knew what he spoke about. This was often infuriating to those of us who were utterly convinced that he knew next to nothing about many topics, but he always wanted the last word.

He would always claim prior knowledge, even in such trivial subjects as film. No matter how critically acclaimed a current release was, he felt that it suffered in comparison with the "original." *A Star Is Born* with Judy Garland and James Mason was fine, yes, but you should have seen the original with Janet Gaynor and Fredric March. The most recent versions of *Back Street* or *Madame X* were "not a patch" on the original black and white versions. The chariot race in *Ben-Hur* was something to behold, especially when Ramon Novarro, rather than Charlton Heston, was at the reins. And even *Gone With the Wind* with Leigh and Gable couldn't measure up to the original..."The original, before 1939?" one would inquire incredulously. "Oh, yes. There was one...with I can't remember who...and it was in black and white."

That was precisely the problem with him: his world was one of black and white, clear-cut options and verdicts.

This quarrelsome habit, this "know-it-all" attitude had ethnic roots. As David Marshall Lang writes in *Armenia: Cradle Of Civilization*: "An Armenian officer in the old Ottoman army once remarked that he preferred to be in charge of a battalion of Turks than one made up of his fellow Armenians: the Turks obeyed without question, but each Armenian would have his own ingenious plan of campaign, and none would attack until they had all been discussed and tried out."

My father diverged from this pattern in one important regard: he was not much given to open discussion; he could be rashly aggressive.

The fiery Armenian temperament is no myth. It finds expression in the popular epic, *David of Sassoun, or Sassna Dzourer (The Daredevils of Sassoun)*. Leon Surmelian, noted translator of the work, explains that *dzour* means "twisted," "mad," "cracked," or even "wacky," but with overtones of courage and heroism, of reckless adventurousness.

From Surmelian's translation:

> The Armenian is *dzour* to begin with, he is mad, and he has survived by breaking the rules of history. He is a wild rebel by nature, a wild rebel with a

dream. In Armenia we have the Don Quixote of nations.

I'm not certain the Quixotan image is appropriate to the Armenian, but the rest fits.

My father had three layers of wildness. The first was powerfully masculine; the second, veiled, nurturingly feminine; and the third, a deep, unprobed source of his essence. The second layer, as delineated in this primal psychic pattern, possessed softer, caring, emotional qualities. My father was generous to a fault with children, strangers, and hangers-on–his family often felt he was an easy touch for those looking for a handout or for those so-called friends who accepted his largesse without ever intending reciprocation–and he was capable of sensitive feeling, but his wild energy too often moved to the surface, swamping softness, and rendering him a male bully.

Was death an unwanted reminder of a final stock-taking that he needed to refuse?

If I ask: 'Are you ready to die?'
He will answer: 'Not yet. My fire is cold ash
But I prefer this over death.
By this I gain revenge,
Persist, endure,
Overwhelm and outlive
The hunters who trapped my child's heart
In a savage cage
Then threw away the key
To the end of an unmarked well.'

My father had been marked for life and so helplessly entangled in a laocoon of Turkish atrocity that he could not recognize my boyhood needs. There was no bonding between us except in times of pain and mourning.

He was a boy who lived past eight decades, but he was a man unable to be a boy who could play without a gnawing hunger in his stomach, a raw taste in his mouth. He loved to eat as if in fear of reprising the starvation of his boyhood, the hunt for wild grass and discarded scraps from tables that never called him to dinner. And even as he gorged himself on rich food in his adult years, extravagant rice dishes with meat, raisins, and almonds, buttery chicken, cool cucumber with yogurt, he could still smell the stench of rotting corpses–those flung into yawning pits or the swollen, waterlogged ones spewed out by the dark sea.

His hunger was the result of nightmare, a delirium moaning like the tide or Ararat levelled by a seismic God.

MASIS

Armenians are linked inextricably to the image of Ararat. It is their sacred mountain, just as Meru is for Indians or Gerizim is for Palestinians. In sacred mythology, mountains are the *axis mundi*, just as trees, pillars, and ladders are. A sacred mountain connects earth and heaven, and so marks the highest point in the world. Consequently, the land that surrounds it is considered the highest among countries. No wonder Ararat harboured Noah's ark.

"Masis," which is what Armenians call their mountain, is really two summits, a smaller one attached to a greater. Ararat proper reaches some 17,000 feet. Visible from many parts of Soviet Armenia, it is really located within Turkish borders, a fact that provokes mixed feelings of frustration and national pride within Armenians. Mount Ararat takes on the dimensions of a gigantic pyramid or temple. Even physically and of itself, it is legendary without the Old Testament's help.

THIRTEEN WAYS OF LOOKING AT A TURK

1

Among Great and Little Ararat,
Broad-shouldered domes,
Was the cry of the Turk.

2

I am of two minds about the Turk
Like Ararat
Where a great chasm runs
Far into its own heart.

3

If we cannot define the Turk
It is only because we don't know him too well.
I wheel around two propositions:
Ataturk's "He's a lucky man who can say
'I am a Turk'"
And his lapidary phrase:
"We resemble ourselves."

4

The Turk has been a slaughterer
Pouring out death in innumerable buckets.

5

I do not know which to prefer–

The proud declamation:
"We are a nation of many enemies"
Or the coded innuendo:
"Take care of the Armenians."
I do not know which to prefer–
The Turk's concept of honour
Or of his kinship.

6

In a Turkish feud, fathers often get
Their young sons to do the deed for them.
If a grown Turk kills, he may be hanged;
But a boy goes to reform school and learns a trade.
Sometimes a tourist feels queasy
Thinking of the other job those hands did
That also made his boots.

7

O poets of Anatolia
Why do you imagine golden birds?
Do you not see how the Turk
Sings with his sword?

8

The sand is moving.
The Turk is afoot.

9

It was night all day.
Shadowed killers
Rousing sleepers to bloody death.
The Turk straddled dismembered limbs.

10

At the sight of the Turk
Moving in a green army

Even the summits of Ararat
Would cry out sharply.

11

Remembering the Armenian massacres
My mind whirls like Rumi's:
A spinning dervish
Who dreams of union with God
Unlike the Turk who is an adept,
My whirling is not a show for tourists.

12

In the *hammam*, dank and dark,
The Turk blooms: his wet body
A steam-kissed pink flower,
Chest anointed,
Legs polished
By stones from a river
Whose far-off water sounds
Drowned chimes for corpses.

13

I know old griefs
And lucid, inescapable reasons:
But I know, too,
That the Turk is involved
In what I know.

IN TRANSLATION

The Turkish part of his history made him feel pursued. By a terror of decay, disease, and death. The body could be a betrayal.

In the midst of his paranoia, there was sometimes fierce comedy.

He was always on the alert for disease, checking himself regularly for skin eruptions, bowel complications, muscle distress. As far as his own body was concerned, he felt there was always a problem incubating. As a young man, he had been muscular and possessed of great stamina, but in his middle years, his muscle tone declined as he took to heavy drinking. He paid the price one evening by slipping down a winding metal staircase and breaking his fall by a firm smash of his elbow. This did, indeed, break his fall, but it also dislocated one of the discs in his neck and left him with chronic pain. He had to use a brace and undertake daily therapy in a harness that was suspended to a beam in the house. At such times, he looked like a man about to be hanged.

"Don't feel sorry for him," my mother used to say. "He'll outlive us all."

He was always reading medical reports in newspapers and magazines about new diseases. Then he would examine himself for symptoms and worry about possible remedies.

"I think I have something in my stomach."

It's probably indigestion, he was told.

"No. I know indigestion. This is something else. Serious. I feel bloated. And I have pain."

But he didn't have any fever, any discoloration, any hard lumps or discharges–which didn't arrest his anxiety. He dreamed of acute suffering, created a scenario of emergency surgery, worried about how he would recuperate.

"He's probably imagining things again," my mother remarked.

Unable to win her concern, much less her sympathy, he took himself to the doctor. Upon his return, my mother asked: "Well, what did the doctor find?"

Sheepishly, my father admitted: "I've got chronic constipation."

The comic anti-climax did not put an end to his hypochondria.

In this regard, my father was made for satire.

In all other matters, he liked to give advice. Even when it was unwanted. And it was usually linked to his paranoia.

If your car had a problem, he would insist that anything your trusted mechanic said was false. "Ech, damn rogues! All of them!" he would scoff. "Don't forget, I know the business."

Everybody, it seemed, was out to "get" him. My brother-in-law, Peter Newton, substantiates this: "He was very distrustful of stores and the government. He thought they were overcharging him with prices and taxes." He would always look at the negative rather than the positive side of things.

If you were thinking of buying a house, he would warn you to beware of the agent. "They'll take your money and run."

If there was an advertised special on footwear, he would claim to know which store had the best article. "Go to my closet and you'll find a nice pair I just bought at Eaton's. Genuine leather. Very comfortable." But why were there so many unused pairs in the closet? "My damned feet are swollen." Go to a doctor, he was told.

"Damn quacks!" he would swear. "It's just bad circulation, they tell me, but there's something wrong. I can feel it. Maybe I should see a specialist." But, according to him, the specialists in Brampton weren't reliable; maybe he should see someone in Toronto. That would necessitate a cab, which cost too much. Maybe he should go to a specialist in Brampton, after all. A doctor was respected only if he confirmed my father's worst fears.

For an Armenian, he had an extraordinary propensity for solutions.

My father forgot how to read Armenian. Anything he read about his homeland was read in translation.

A pity that he died without having read Vahan Tekeyan, the soneteer of perfect pitch, who told us what "we shall say to God":

> let us swear that when we find
> God in his paradise offering comfort
> to make amends for our pain,
> let us swear that we will refuse
> saying No, send us to hell again.
> We choose hell. You made us know it well.
> Keep your paradise for the Turk.

This poetry does not read well in translation.

When Marzbed Margossian and Diana Der Hovanessian wanted to put together an anthology of Armenian poetry, their mothers offered conflicting advice. One said: "Hurry and do it." The other: "Don't do it. The Armenian alphabet was invented to keep our poetry to ourselves."

My father often lived his life as if keeping something all to himself.

My father never taught his three children Armenian. So his language is a barren orchard I have never walked in, a ruined palace whose corridors I have never traversed, a vast country whose storms I have not weathered.

In one sense, I am writing all this to myself.

There is some significance in the fact that he was named Adam, though I believe he had his own views on Original Sin.

For him the fall of man was dated April 24, 1915.

This memoir must be a monument in a time difficult for monuments.

"If you want to rise above your time let the past hoist you up."
– EGHISHE CHARENTS (1897-1937)

I wish these white pages could be a dove fluttering with news of a covenant.

But time was a rope looped around the neck of my father, and in his dark eyes I saw the bottom of a canyon.

In my childhood I made my father a legend. I used to tell visitors that the breadknife was really the weapon he once used to kill a tiger.

None of us had ever seen a live tiger except in a circus or zoo.

I once knew a woman who had Arab lovers though her daughter's boyfriend was an Israeli Jew.

It is possible to take sides and still love those whom history decrees are your enemies.

I have taught English to young Turks, and I have been utterly courteous.

I hope, when they are grown, they will remember me as one who did not include them in his inventory of revenge. I hope, however, that they did not mistake my politeness for forgiveness.

Perhaps there was no sense in my truce. Certainly their presence made no sense of the past. Certainly my diplomacy brought no confidence in tomorrow.

As poets say, the Armenian language is a home for a wandering, dispersed tribe, and as my father lost most of this language, he became an urchin again, without his own roof, walls, and doorways.

What does this make me–the son of an urchin–who speaks no Armenian?

Because I harboured anger at my father, I refused to learn Armenian. I refused to attend Armenian class, even when it became available to me.

Once I deliberately lost a beautiful, jewelled ring crafted especially for me by an Armenian family friend, Leon Sanossian.

I did not want any identification with my father's tribe, even though I loved that jeweller and his plump, short wife, Baidzer, who served adults pastries and tea from a silver samovar, joked, called us children "dollinks," and read our tea leaves.

Armenians have a long history of superstitions, despite the fact that they were discouraged from believing in ancient practices, rituals, and omens by church leaders.

Superstition helped them in times when they could have succumbed to affliction.

From a land of great masses of rock and mountain, they believed in stone.

Stone made the earth strong.

After removing stones from a field, villagers would stack them carefully in the belief that to remove the stone entirely would weaken the earth.

Stone also made for fertility.

A barren tree could be turned fruitful if a stone were placed in its fork.

Some stones could bring milk to the sallow breasts of dry women.

Superstition sustained the people, sometimes in the most bizarre ways.

In times of drought, a woman could be yoked to a plow which dug a furrow in the dry earth. This helped produce rain.

My father never mentioned these ancient practices or the one I recently read about in a study of Armenian peasants–about the reliable method of bringing rain by cutting off the head from a Turkish corpse and throwing it into a river.

In a variant version, villagers exhumed a corpse, cut off the skull, and sprinkled water on it because it was believed that the newly dead were thirsty. Let the living satisfy the dead; perhaps, God would then satisfy the living.

I remember my father's death grimace, his mouth open in a silent, parched cry.

There was one superstition he did have. My sister, Elma, who was named after his mother, Elmas, was dearly beloved by him. Her name was an English variant for the Armenian word for "pearl." A pearl was something precious hidden in a shell. It had something mystical about it, being in the center of obscurity. A pearl was believed to transfigure infirmity or abnormality. I seriously doubt that my parents understood all the symbolism. Elma was simply named in loving remembrance of my father's tragicallyfated mother. As a young girl, Elma was given pearl earrings by our Armenian friends, the Sanossians, in the hope that this gift would be emblematic of her name and good fortune. Shortly after receiving the gift, however, Elma suffered a grave illness. Convinced that the pearls had something to do with this bad luck, my parents threw the earrings away and swore for the rest of their lives that pearls were unlucky.

LETTING OUT THE CAGED BIRD SLOWLY

In thinking about a style for this memoir, I have been drawn to the terse, epigrammatic mode. To some this will seem underdeveloped. But the bias to "develop" reminds me of Octavio Paz's image of "a frantic race to arrive at the gates of Hell ahead of everyone else."

The writer wears a mask, and for each book the mask changes.
Here my mask is of a quester.
In Latin my quest would be a form of inquiry.
In Spanish my quest would be a form of desire or love.
I do not yet know what my quest is in my father's tongue.

Paz claims that language is the mark or sign, not of man's fall but of his original innocence. "Through the Word we may regain the lost kingdom..."

Once in my teenage years, I did not speak to my father for months, the result of some indignity he had visited upon me. I even refused to be driven to school by him, electing to walk over a mile and a half each morning, regardless of the elements.

"Why doesn't he speak to me?" he would complain angrily. "I am his father. He must respect me."

The more he demanded respect, the more I resisted to effect a truce. This state of things made for a sullen drama, something like that in Atom Egoyan's otherwise satirical *Next of Kin* where an unrepentant Armenian daughter clashes with her father on questions of values.

My mother fretted quietly and moved slowly and nervously about our home. Close family friends counselled me to make peace.

To speak to him before his apology, I felt, was to betray my own sensitivity by using words that were too personal.

My style is my behaviour with language.

I like to believe that this style is open, not closed, to let a certain bird out of its cage. But the bird is let out slowly.

WATER EPISODES

And yet my words can sometimes flow like water.

"In the Vedas, water is referred to as *matritamah* (the most maternal) because, in the beginning, everything was like a sea without light."

– J.E. CIRLOT, *DICTIONARY OF SYMBOLS*

A secondary meaning of the symbol is intuitive wisdom. For the Mesopotamians, the abyss of water was a symbol of unfathomable Wisdom.

I regard myself as a perennial swimmer.

> Some of my strongest childhood memories are of brooks in Khandala, where I cupped my hands in the very shallows where village cows drank, and caught tiny rock-fish, slender, translucent, yet hardy creatures that survived longer than any goldfish in a bowl;
>
> Juhu Beach in Bombay, where I once saw a giant liver-brown stingray flopping on the littered sand, and where *fakirs* often buried themselves up to their necks as a yoga exercise, and where often it was impossible to swim because of the pounding grey-green waves, perfidious jellyfish, and saboteur undertows;
>
> Marine Drive, where my mother gorged herself on *bhel puri, batata puri, pani puri,* tamarind sauce, and pistachio *kulfi*, and where important politicians addressed the thronging crowds through loudspeakers;
>
> and Back Bay, a salt-water swimming pool at Marine Beach, where an older cousin had to pull me up by the hair on my head after I had plunged into the deep end without knowing how to swim.

Despite that foolish plunge, I have not feared water, except when I pass over it by aeroplane, or on long voyages by steamship, where the multitudinous seas look too deep for comfort.

I have always felt instinctively the symbolism of water: its significance as (what Eliade calls) "the universal sum of virtualities." Water is *fons et origo*, the "spring and origin," the "reservoir," says Eliade, of "all the possibilities of existence."

My father did play a role in some of my childhood water episodes. When he drove us to Juhu, my sisters and I would be fully changed into our swimwear even before the car was parked. The three of us would scoot through the sand towards the foam, ignoring all parental concern for our safety.

At the end of the swim, he would have to keep chasing us out of the water, one by one, but every time he managed to carry one of us on to shore, the other two would dash back to the surf or stand, toes dug into the sand which seemed to recede with the ebb of the sea.

There is a picture of him, crouched on his haunches, nestling me to him in the foaming shallows. I am wearing a two-year old's one-piece beach-wear with an embroidered animal over the chest. It seems to be a lion motif.

My mother is directly behind my father. She wears sun-glasses and a maternity dress, as she was pregnant with my sister Elma, born two years after me.

It is a black and white photograph, with dark-skinned Johnny Condor (my father's best man at his wedding) and the fair-skinned Stellas and Oscars, Portuguese friends who all ended up in Australia some years later.

It is a pleasant picnic picture. My friend Alan is smiling as his mother, sprawled in the ankle-deep water, clutches him to her. Mrs. Stella holds towels and sun-hats off to the right as one hand gently holds up her dress just above the knees.

My father is the only one turned away from the camera. He looks off to his right as though he were a little uncomfortable holding me.

Actually he is not really holding me. His stocky arms form brackets around my small body, but they barely touch me.

But this may not be indifference. It could be his peculiar form of gentleness.

I remember my father bobbing in the sea, helping to direct a huge rubber tube on which my mother lay nervously. She had an irremediable fear of water.

A single wave broke his grasp of the tube and capsized my mother.

After her spasms of desperate coughing, she never again trusted my father near water.

A photograph is our possession of the world by a small segment.

A photograph, as Roy Kiyooka says, returns an image to the world.

A photograph is a re-statement of the real.

A memoir is literary photography.

Susan Sontag claims that photography is "an elegiac art, a twilight art."

There is another curious photograph of my father. In this one, he poses with a bicycle at the side of our home.

I know this is a posture of mind in relation to an audience.

My father was not a rider of bicycles.

REPROACH

What is it about a father's criticism that makes it so powerful, able to break down the order you need, within and outside yourself? It is like lightning at first–sky-splitting, palpable, pure and uncontrived–then like low rumblings of thunder, reproachful even in retrospect, generated out of a need to be insistent, a need to lacerate you inside your skull. It does not permit escape. You are shut up within its mockery, and no matter how you try to seek shelter under a pillow or between the pages of a book, you can hear the vibrations passing through the calm details of your sought-after refuge.

That I felt urged to sing at my cousin Neville's wedding was my choice, though not so much a choice really, but a spontaneous impulse born out of love for him.

We had been at the same school, though he was far senior to me, and I had thrilled at his skill at cricket. An all-rounder, he bowled (medium-pace) and batted left-handed with the fluent grace of a Neil Harvey and the power of a Gary Sobers, though he himself was no admirer of the West Indian Sobers, whom he accused of being an unorthodox "crossbat." Neville's drives were a joy to watch, as he swung his bat in a long sweeping arc that sent the ball whizzing past flummoxed fielders towards the boundary. His footwork was as nimble as a dancer's, and his square-cuts and pulls to leg were executed with confident ease rather than accidental slickness. His bowling, too, was lyrical, as he approached the crease in long, loping strides that gathered momentum, before he hurled the ball that cut across a batsman's waist and dipped in a sudden red flash.

Neville was tall, slim, and shy. Though he excelled at sports, he was modest, and his conversation was marked by a stutter. Not having a brother, I was proud to bond with him. He was an older cousin who would look out for me in the schoolyard where I was prone to get into wrestling matches with peers.

After school, he found a lucrative job in the Persian Gulf where his cricket prowess was lauded by his English, Australian, and American co-workers. But his heart pined for home and Joyce, his beloved, tall, slender, and the colour of cloves, and not all the money in Arabia could stop his return home. I exulted.

As the wedding couple walked down the aisle after the service, blooming in everybody's attention, I was happy for them, joining in the fuss and laughter about getting Joyce's train neatly arranged in the limousine, and at the reception in a spacious hall, I even put aside my adolescent self-consciousness to dance with my mother. The elementary box-step she had taught me served passably well. I managed to glide and pause, turn and repeat the learned sequence without counting out aloud.

I did not notice my father's progressive inebriation. Indeed, I did not need to, for it was a foregone conclusion that as the evening wore on in its full flush of cordiality, he would take immoderate advantage of the bar. And then, of course, would come his uninhibited revelry: botched attempts at jokes in a furry voice, his clumsy attempts at the slow fox-trot which would have defied all the remediation of an Arthur Murray, and the eventual displacement of his robust good cheer by a sour truculence. Drink provoked his distemper.

At the height of festivity, the band played requests, and Joyce serenaded her husband with a rendition of "All The Way." Her voice had a pleasant, though slightly unmusical, composure, but only those with self-assured malice would have cavilled. The lyric and the personal emotion with which she invested it transcended the flaws. The song had a soothing sweetness, a bright hopefulness, as if the complications of the newlyweds' adventures could be simply enfolded in love's gentleness.

A sudden impulse took me. I was standing near the podium, and when Joyce finished to a hearty round of applause, more striking of spoons against wine-glasses and cries of "Kiss! Kiss!", I made a split-second decision.

There was no need to show off this time, though I was known for my parlour performances–a recitation from Shakespeare or Dickens, a comic impression of an Indian speaking *babu* English ("My wife and I have trouble making both our ends meet"), or a transvestite monologue as an Anglo-Indian *memsahib* making gossip over the phone. I was a performer, though much less self-assured than many believed.

I heard myself saying to the bandleader, "May I have the microphone, please?" The words seemed to have been muffled in a fog. That I had never sung publicly before, that perhaps I was not on fully intimate terms with a complete song lyric–these thoughts never entered my mind. I was surprised by my own risk-taking. The microphone cord trailed around me like a live body, coiling and stretching, unpredictable but finally familiar, and I was there on the podium, where I'd wanted to be, though not quite certain of what I would do to carry off this daring gesture.

I do not remember the song's title. I can only remember dedicating the song to the happy couple, and the first bars deceived the audience into thinking that I was in control of the situation.

Then my mind went blank–as if struck by a blinding flash, a punishment for my preposterous presumption. Nothing could help, not the bandleader's gentle cueing or the audience's coaxing applause. My impetuous pleasure evaporated into edgy embarrassment. I felt dizzy and unanchored, and I stumbled to my seat, dazed by my own self-destruction.

Everybody tried to console me with words that applauded my courage and motive. Everybody told me to forget the incident.

My father, however, couldn't wait to disapprove. He watched me the rest of the night with a stalker's eyes. He became a streak of hate, pure meanness, like the glint of a blade, and all the long way home, he repeated his damning mockery. "You had to make a fool of yourself? You couldn't even remember the words!"

Somehow he contrived to view the episode through a peculiar focus. He was embarrassed for himself, not for me, and the public nature of this embarrassment enflamed him. Somehow my failure was a verdict on him and our family.

For once, I did not retaliate. I felt a sense of despair and the destruction of any love that remained for him.

I wish I did not remember this. I wish the incident would fall away like the forgotten title of that aborted song in the middle of a golden night, breathing love for my cousin, as the confetti and crêpe streamers, the cut-flowers and table-decorations continue glowing in what can only be a hoped-for, fervent, forgiving hush.

Perhaps I am distorting the truth of my father. Perhaps he was not quite the casually cruel man I perceived him to be at certain moments in my life.

And yet...

My sister Audrey refused to contribute any memories of or reflections on my father. I had thought that she was upset over my quest for truth, my intrusion into private family matters. But I was to learn a different truth about her some months into the battle with my Kenoran second wife over claims of assets and property. She called as peace-maker, attempting to allay my storms of fury, but she prefaced her urgings with this remark: "You know why I didn't have anything to offer about Daddy? I can't find anything good to say about him. You don't know the vile things he said about me and Peter about trying to swindle him out of Elma's estate."

She had always been discreetly reticent about private matters, and the rotting field of his mind had forced her to immure her revulsion deep within her silence.

But now I knew, I knew. His paranoid attacks on family had always infuriated me. Nevertheless, I was shocked by my sister's sudden revelation of her hitherto unvoiced feelings.

There were close family friends who never knew or who, if they did, refused to acknowledge this shameful part of his nature.

When Lesley Kulhanian, whose Armenian father, Ardash, was about ten years older than mine, sent me a letter from Vancouver in December, 1998, it gave me another perspective. Her father, who had been born in Istanbul where his own father had been a prominent stage actor, met mine at the Armenian church in Bombay, sometime in the late thirties. My father made an ineradicable impression on the Kulhanian family with his memories of the genocide. By the time he had met and married my mother, he was earning a good wage as Manager of French Motor Company, and apparently he spoilt his wife and three children, "giving them whatever they wanted and denying them nothing." Lesley's letter startled me by its angle of vision, offering a revision of my own impressions, so I quote at length:

> He said he wanted [you all] to have everything that he had missed out on. My parents and close friends told him he was being foolish, but he loved his family and would do anything for them. However, although he was generous in the housekeeping money he gave your mother, he was prudent enough to save something every month from his paycheque which stood him in good stead when the family

> immigrated to Canada. As you well know, your mother was very generous and spent what she was given with no regard for the future. Life was good in India and your father never did begrudge lavishing his money and his love and affection on his family as they were very important to him.

The new images pierce my heart: my mother is portrayed as an unconscionable spendthrift, my father as a poignant soul, generous to a fault. I recall only that my father sent us away for a month's vacation in a cool hill-station such as Matheran or Panchgani when the humidity and heat of Bombay became intolerable. We were served three meals a day by liveried waiters, took hikes in the country in quest of wild berries, sometimes had the pampered luxury of rickshaw, *tonga*, or pony rides, and passed the evening hours with bingo, snakes-and-ladders, or draughts. My mother preferred bridge, and her indulgence came to the fore in Bombay where she was part of The Retreat bridge-set or when she visited friends at the appropriately-named Readymoney Building. She also liked the occasional bet at the Mahim racetrack, but she was never a big gambler.

Then the letter shifts to the Garebians in Canada:

> Although your parents knew that both of them would have to go to work, it broke your father's heart to have his wife go to work as he had always been able to support his family. Neither of them were [sic] very successful in landing jobs right away, and it was some time before your mother got into Rolls Royce, and your father also could have landed a good position in the same firm except that the company had the archaic policy of not permitting more than one member of a family to work for the firm, and so he lost out on a good opportunity.

The letter sketches in quick detail some of the Canadian travails of my father. Determined to maintain something similar to the standard of life his family had enjoyed in Bombay, he wanted his wife to remain mistress of the home while he sought employment:

> In his line in Quebec it was not easy as most of the mechanics were French Canadian and his lack of the French language was a drawback. He had the highest mechanical certification, but dropped to a lower certification as no one was prepared to hire him at the rate he would have commanded at the higher level. Work was sporadic for him as is the case in certain fields of employment, and he returned to India to start up his own business which would prove lucrative, and he would be able to send funds to Canada and ensure that his wife would not have to go out to work. However, your father was a family man and wanted to be with his family and not be miles away, so he returned to Canada and plodded on with the jobs that came his way. You must appreciate that with the incoming cash flow being drastically reduced, there had to be financial restraints, and a bit of belt tightening. This came as a shock to the children who had been spoilt over the years, and I am sure was hard to adjust to.

More startling imagery. My sisters and I are clearly seen as having been spoilt and plaintive. This does not sort with my own memory, but then if you are spoilt, you probably would not recognize yourself as such.

The letter, which is clearly a testimonial to my deceased father, continues:

> Keith, your father never changed, but if he did not take care of the funds...if there were no restraints the family could have gone bankrupt, and then what would have happened!!

The punctuation is signal: the coordinate clause is more a thunderclap assertion than a rhetorical question. My father is clearly evoked in sentimental fashion, but the emotion is genuine. What rankles me, however, is the almost one-sided sympathy that makes this version virtually subversive as far as my own impressions are concerned.

> Remember your father came to Canada at age 50 years, and it is not easy at that age to find employment. Besides he started having health problems with arthritis in his shoulder, but he still went out on the midnight shift to repair broken snow removal equipment in the cold sub zero weather. He worked for as long as he possibly could under these conditions, and in the end had to quit because he was unable to perform the job because of his painful shoulders. Your father, Keith, was a man to whom family meant a great deal and he provided for his family as best he could, because he regretted so much never having had a family when he was growing up. He was not a selfish man and whatever he did was for his family. Your mother was easy going and was the last of the big time spenders, and your father indulged her....Your father was a good man and ready to help others [.][H]is outlook on life was that family came first above all else, and he lived and died by that rule.

The Kulhanian testimonial is doubly touching. I am moved by Lesley's loyalty to my father's memory and her evident love for his valiant spirit. And I am stirred by something else, something that rebounds within myself. Am I disloyal to his memory by being so critical of his failings? Am I an ingrate? Do I lack an objective perspective of myself and my own family, having been wounded, perhaps beyond Lesley's knowledge, by his paranoid spasms of anger?

Or is Lesley missing something vital? Family feeling, financial restraint, toil and travail are all worthy things that need to be praised and remembered, but there are other things in a life that make generalizations hazardous. I can summon up only the father I experienced, however incomplete that image may be to other witnesses.

The Kulhanian version, whatever its sympathies and implied criticisms, cannot be rejected. It pins down some of the positive qualities of my father, and paradoxically brings me closer to him even as I struggle to resist the epistle's judgements of my mother, my younger sisters, and me in Bombay.

My father's life in my memoir can be imagined as a palimpsest, the letter from Vancouver being one more piece of handwriting placed over other fragmentary versions of his life. The letter does not quite erase what I have written; it simply adds to it.

Does this make memoir-writing a twilight craft? The hidden becomes partially visible in a faint light. And what is seen in the lovely faintness cleans itself with words that have a talismanic charm: *generous*, *prudent*, *family*, *a good man*.

And I can remember moments which support this side of him. "He was always there for us when we needed him," comments my brother-n-law who, perhaps more than anybody else, bore the brunt of my father's paranoia and manipulativeness. My father was shaken by my first divorce, principally because he felt for my son and for me. "Does Michael ever call you? Do you see him?" he would inquire. "Do you stay in touch with his mother?" His was an unspoken hope that my son and I would never drift apart. He also wanted me to have an amicable relationship with my ex-wife. This was inherently noble of him.

I touch the thin, neatly folded, typewritten letter. I touch a part of my dead father.

JUMBLED NIGHTMARE

One of the fascinations of a memoir is to get a true story.

Nearly a month after my mother's death, after he had taken me to a leisurely lunch of clams, shrimp, and sole, where he benumbed himself with two glasses of red wine, my father surprised me by divulging part of his story.

I did not have to press him much to begin. "I need to know certain facts about your life."

I expected uneasiness, suspicion, awkward hesitation. Instead, I got a calmly told, though jumbled, nightmare.

My father was born on December 26, 1909 in Dekranaget Sun in the province of Diyarbekir, a land memorialized by King Dekran or, as he is commonly called, Tigranes the Great who is largely known to us from the annals of his Roman foes or from magnificent silver coinage that he grandly commissioned. This ruler ascended the throne in 95 B.C. as the Roman power in Asia Minor was being shaken by Mithridates Eupator, King of Pontus, who threatened to drive the Romans out of Asia altogether. Tigranes, ever the shrewd opportunist, entered into an alliance with Mithridates and married his thirteen-year old daughter, Cleopatra. Tigranes was immensely ambitious and exercised his military power by defeating several other kings. After victories against the Romans, Parthians, the Seleucids, Cilicians, and Phoenicians, he united all the territories inhabited by Armenians. Syria fell to him, and he was able to advance into northern Palestine. Power certainly inflated his ego, and he assumed the grand title of "King of Kings," before deciding that this needed to be magnified to "God" or "the Divine." Tigranes' kingdom extended from the Caspian Sea to the Mediterranean, from Mesopotamia to the Pontic Alps. His capital, Tigranokerta, was massively impressive. Surrounded by a wall fifty cubits high, wide and thick enough for equine stables to be built within, it boasted a royal palace not far outside, a fortified castle nearby, and parks for hunting or ponds for fishing. Intended to be a centre of Hellenistic science, art, and literature, it was a real showplace.

However, this King of Kings was obviously guilty of *hubris*, and eventually he faced military defeat by the Romans, as well as rebellion by one of his sons.

A very Armenian story in that Tigranes' life deteriorated into a chronicle of turbulent upheaval, family dissension, and humiliation. He to whom many other regents were forced to pay tribute had to depend on the final kindness of his Roman subjugators.

When recalling the name and glory of Tigranes, my father neglected to relate the reductive fate of the King of Kings.

"I was born in a region made famous by King Dekran," he proudly related to me.

His father, Stephen, was from a family of iron manufacturers who specialized in tools and machinery for irrigation and agriculture. He was suddenly "recruited" into the Turkish army and disappeared forever in a convoy to the front.

My father's mother was named Elmas (later incorrectly transformed on his British passport into Elma).

"What did she look like?" I asked.

"Exactly like your sister Elma."

My father was the second of four children, all the others being girls: Rose (Varti), older than him by about four years; another, whose name he could not remember; and the youngest, Arshe, who was about four years younger than him and who had beautiful curly hair.

Just before Easter in 1915, his world fell apart.

Before dusk when Turkish *muezzins* called Muslims to prayer, the streets teemed. Kurds drove carts of melons to the bazaar, gendarmes rode on horseback, women shouldering amphoras met at fountains to exchange gossip and scandal, old storytellers in the marketplace sucked words from ancient waterpipes, the outdoor cafés filled with tea-drinkers who often played cards or backgammon as vendors offered *simit*, sesame rings on sticks. Food and drink were part of daily commerce. *Raki*, like Greek *ouzo*, a strong, clear liquor that turned milky when ice or water was added. Multicoloured fresh fish on crimson trays. *Shish kebab*, yogurt, and *lokum* for those with a sweet tooth.

The Armenians met and talked the way they always talked, excitedly, incessantly, until it was time to return to their wide-eaved houses with red-tiled roofs.

At dusk, the Muslim call to prayer was a secret semaphore, a coded message for sanctioned terror.

In small villages or cities, across Anatolia, the Turks beat on every Armenian family's doors, ordering the occupants to leave all their possessions just where they were. Women were dragged out of washtubs, children snatched from their beds. On the mountainsides, where poplars latticed the sky, farmers were forced to leave their ploughs and cattle and join the "deportation." The Turks forbade the taking of any photographs of this "deportation" on pain of death, though a few brave German missionaries did manage a hurried picture or two through hotel windows. As mule-carts rumbled along the route, and as the convoys of thousands of helpless Armenians were reduced to shuffling bundles of rags, the Turks organized special bands of criminals and Kurdish tribesmen who preyed on the defenceless columns. Women and children were raped, men and youth disappeared. The Turks pretended that the males were recruits for their army, but many bodies were later discovered in ditches. The Kurds had a propensity for slicing off breasts and hands with scimitars and flinging babies into burning bushes. Stray dogs had a rich feast on human carrion, scattering bones about.

My father was part of a horde of children who marched into a compound where mounted soldiers bore swords glinting in the sun. The children remained in terror for hours, until the *mufti* or chief priest appeared and prevented the soldiers from executing them.

The next day all the mothers and children were forced out of the town. "Don't lock your doors! Take only what you're wearing!" they were ordered. There was a war coming.

In truth, the war had been planned in secrecy following the entrenchment of Enver, Talaat, and Djemel as unchallenged dictators of Turkey after their *coup* of January 26, 1913. The triumvirate had learned their lessons in ferocity from excellent masters. Before becoming Minister of War, Enver, a diminutive man who walked on tiptoe and who had long, girlish eyelashes, had been Ottoman Military Attaché in Berlin between 1909 and 1911 where he had learned to speak fluent German and, as David Marshall Lang informs us in *The Armenians (A People in Exile)*, he had been an "undisguised admirer of Prussian militarism," going so far, despite certain soft physical traits, as to identify physically with Kaiser Wilhelm in the form of a moustache, "sharply turned up at the ends." Described as a "dainty war god," he gave rise to hundreds of boastful stories about his mad daring. He once stood, cigarette in mouth, before the howitzer muzzle of mutineers, challenging them to pull the firing-cord. Djemel, once a colonel in the Turkish Third Army, was a warrior who led even whirling dervishes into battle. He became Minister of the Marine. Black moustached, mighty-headed Talaat, Minister of the Interior, was grey at the temples, had a fat double chin, jutting belly, and massive hands (twice the size of an ordinary person's), and, like his partners, had been one of the Young Turks, fanatical soldiers who had surpassed the cruelty of Sultan Abdul-Hamid II. At first, the Armenians had welcomed the triumvirate's deposition of Hamidian atrocity. After all, Hamid had begun the Armenian genocide in 1895, exercising a repertoire of executions by firing squad, decapitation with cavalry sword, or hanging. Turkish mobs were allowed to seize and kill recalcitrant Armenians by any way they conjured. It has been estimated that within two years, some three hundred thousand Armenians were put to death.

There was neither sanctuary nor mercy for any Armenian in the path of a Turkish mob. It was useless to seek Christian churches for refuge; the mob merely barricaded the doors and set fire to the buildings, trapping most of the hapless in a raging conflagration and then leaping onto the few who desperately sought to break out.

To be an Armenian in Islamic Turkey was to be in the wrong place. Armenians were resented because they were an élite: they were the brains and vitality of Turkey, being lawyers, doctors, merchants, metalworkers, skilled craftsmen. Most foreign trade was conducted by Armenians. The provision of raw materials and manufactured goods was managed by Armenian firms that had European branches. A thousand years before the Turks seized power, Armenians had been industrious peasants who turned the region into a prosperous one. In the interior, Armenian agricultural methods in Anatolia were decades ahead of Turkish small landholdings. Cilician Armenians had imported threshing-machines and steam-ploughs from Europe for agriculture. The Turks smashed the machinery. Following the pattern of any group with an inferiority complex, the Turks resented Armenians for their thriving success. Turkish persecution of Armenian doctors, teachers, engineers, and intellectuals showed a country determined to live without intellect. But their hate needed an excuse for a full-scale eruption, and war provided a convenient one.

As the Ottoman Empire was on the verge of disintegration, the Turks turned to their army. The empire needed a purge, and the Young Turks, founders of a secret political party, were sworn to political and social reform. Ironically, the Young Turks first aligned themselves with the Armenians and other national minorities in order to promote the idea of a liberalized multi-national state under a western model, but the outbreak of World War I changed the empire's course. Turkey supported imperial Germany, and in return the Kaiser armed and trained the Turkish army to imitate the goose-step. The Armenians, unaware at the time that such nationalism and militarism would lead to their own virtual extinction, fought for the Ottoman army. Many of them, however, realized that fellow-Armenians were fighting on the Russian side, which was, of course, the enemy side, as far as Turkey was concerned. The Young Turks, suspicious of potential sabotage, reacted by executing Armenian soldiers and ordering the removal of Armenian civilians from the war zone.

The deportation method, which would be grotesquely enlarged by Hitler in his extermination of the Jews, was learned from the Kaiser and Baron Von Wangenheim who had advocated the evacuation of the Greeks from Smyrna and surrounding areas.

The holocaust of 1915 was preceded by one in 1895, establishing Turkey's fanatical propensity for race-murder.

History records what is called "the autumn killings," mass extermination carried out with a remarkable degree of unconscionable efficiency. Turks looked for the slightest provocation to retaliate against Armenians, who became non-persons (as would the Jews become in Nazi Germany). Villages and cities were torched, Armenian churches knocked down or used as stables or mosques. The historical record is a long, bloody one that no waters of Asia could ever wash clean.

Trebizond, Akhisar, Erzindjan, Bitlis and Gumush-hana, Baiburt, Urfa, Erzerum, Arabkir.

In 1915, the same names appear–with additions. Baku, Maskinah, Zeitun, Erzindjan, Trebizond, Djevdet in Bitlis, Moush and Sasun, Shabin Karahisar, Kharput, Sivas, Angora, Marsovan, Diyarbekir, Musa Dagh, Ras ul-Ain. The names from an incomplete list. Yet enough names of the killing zones to form a litany that hardly anybody recites today. They are difficult names, difficult to pronounce, alien to Western understanding or interest, but they cast a long shadow all the way to Auschwitz.

When Hitler was planning his genocide, he remarked with an unctuous smile: "Who remembers the Armenians now?"

"We have done more to solve the Armenian problem in three months than Abdul Hamid did in thirty years," boasted Talaat Pasha.

To be an Armenian in Islamic Turkey was to be the victim of a racial conspiracy. "Either they disappear, or we do," warned Talaat with fanatical conviction.

There was to be complete extermination, except for a single Armenian corpse to be left as a museum exhibit.

"Take care of the Armenians" was an invidiously euphemistic code.

Taking care of the Armenians reached its apogée with the final phase in April, 1915.

Djevdet Bay, brother-in-law of Enver Pasha, led a disastrous military expedition in northeast Persia. Badly in need of men to replace his slaughtered soldiers, he demanded four thousand Armenians from the region of Van. Armenian leaders offered four hundred and money as an exemption fee for thirty-six hundred. When Bay rejected this, a delegation of four leaders went to negotiate with him on April 16, but were murdered on the way. Three days later, Djevdet Bay issued a proclamation: "The Armenians must be exterminated. If any Muslim protect a Christian, first, his house shall be burned; then the Christian killed before his eyes, then [the Muslim's] family and himself."

The same day, in the village of Akantz close to the Russian border, the entire male population of 2,500 was annihilated.

Armenian males were needed by the Turkish army, but with the proliferation of racist nationalism, Armenian soldiers in this army achieved an uneviable, new status. Stripped of their arms, they were forced to become labourers and pack animals, starved of proper food and abandoned when they fell ill or exhausted.

"On a certain date, in whatever town or village it might be (and the dates show a significant sequence), the public crier went through the streets announcing that every male Armenian must present himself fortwith at the Government Building....The men presented themselves in their working clothes, leaving their shops and work-rooms open, their ploughs in the field, their cattle on the mountain side. When they arrived, they were thrown without explanation into prison, kept there a day or two, and then marched out of the town in batches, roped man to man, along some southerly or south-easterly road. They were starting, they were told, on a long journey–to Mosul or perhaps to Baghdad....They had bidden no farewell to their families....But they had not long to ponder their plight, for they were halted and massacred at the first lonely place on the road." (From the Viscount Bryce-Arnold Toynbee report)

The second part of the phase involved women and children.

The Young Turks showed ingenuity in this part. Instead of massacring their victims outright, they decided to deport them into some desolate wilderness. After all, a proper genocide demanded humiliation as well as murder.

In the oil-rich desert near Deir-es-Zor lay deep, dark caves into which the Armenians were crowded, there to be put to death by slow starvation or to have a quick end by being burned alive. Some managed to hide in tunnels and sustain themselves by eating the burned flesh of their compatriots.

And never was there any remorse by a Turk.

"These things are inevitable," said Talaat with remarkable *sang-froid*.

When pressed for an explanation by a reporter from Berlin, he waxed eloquent: "We have been reproached for making no distinction between the innocent Armenian and the guilty; but that was utterly impossible, in view of the fact that those who were innocent today might be guilty tomorrow."

From the Bryce-Toynbee report:

"After the Armenian men had been summoned away to their death, there was usually a few days' interval in whatever town it might be, and then the crier was heard again in the streets, bidding all Armenians who remained to prepare themselves for deportation, while placards to the same effect were posted on the walls. This applied, in actual fact, to the women and children, and to a poor remnant of the men who, through sickness, infirmity, or age, had escaped the fate marked out for their sex...."

In their self-blinding arrogance, the Turks never counted on Armenian survivors to leave evidence. But there are voices that cry out of the void, voices of those who can speak for the dead.

They speak in memory of those with names and those without.

Some of them are of women holding hands in a circle as Turkish soldiers crack whips across the women's backs, faces, and breasts, shouting insults and ordering them to dance. Which they do while praying together, their cuts and blood-soaked hair turning their near-naked bodies red. Around them are their children, also in a circle, commanded to clap out a rhythm for their mothers' bizarre dance. The Turkish whips do not discriminate between mothers and their young. If they don't clap hard enough, the children are lashed. Two and three-year olds cry uncontrollably. Faster, faster, faster, they are urged.

Then some soldiers with wooden buckets splash kerosene on the dancers and set the women alight with flaming brands. The dancers' feet weave fire on fire. And still the children clap, afraid that they too will be joined to the fire.

Reviewing the television documentary, *The Hidden Holocaust*, I was surprised at how much I had forgotten: that some victims had had horseshoes nailed to the soles of their feet, that mothers who had just given birth had been forced out of bed with time only to snatch a scrap of food and a shawl, that old men had been dragged through the streets, that priests had been crucified on their altars.

What spirit could be found in these places of great degredation? In my father's case, it was a new Adam learning to raise himself from the dead, to begin again.

Are these recreations of nightmare a blasphemy by imagination?

It is possible to imagine sounds to match the images of ragged skeletons, burning villages, marauding Kurds. The brutality of facts cannot afford to go silently into darkness.

It is my duty to imagine.

The Armenians arrived at a cave near a waterfall. At night Turkish soldiers raped the women and young girls. My father remembered a fifteen year old cousin decking a soldier with a single punch and then leaping, with her mother, into a river before the soldier could rise and slay her. That cousin drowned and was carried away by the current; her mother was pinned between rocks, from where she was rescued for further torture.

The soldiers laid a rickety plank across the river, but a young mother, with a six-month baby in her arms, slipped and fell into the water. As she swirled helplessly around, she cried. Nobody could or would do anything for her or her baby.

There were eyewitness reports of other atrocities as well. Men and women would be bound together by rope and pushed into a swelling river. When the Turks shot one of them, the others would also be pulled down by the murdered one to a muddy death.

The Armenians marched without food for almost three days. Fatigued and driven to desperation by starvation and cruelty, my father's mother gave her youngest daughter, Arshe, to a Kurdish farmer and his barren wife.

The second daughter–the nameless one in my father's piecemeal chronicle–was abandoned not long after. Too tired to carry the girl, his mother sat her by a tree and told her not to worry, that she would return to fetch her.

My father's final image of this nameless one is of a five-year old girl, with curly hair, crying by herself beside an inhospitable tree.

"I remember how the Euphrates wound down the descending plateau as we approached it from a distance. It was brown and muddy and thick. Now and then I saw some Kurds out by the banks hawking gazelles, and searching piles of feces for coins. Along the valley paths of the tributaries, corpses began to appear in piles, and as we got closer to the bank near nightfall bloated bodies covered with worms were everywhere. The smell was horrible....Many of the bodies were black from the sun, black tongues hanging out. Emaciated bodies showing a whole skeleton through the decaying skin. The stomachs of pregnant women had been split open, and their unborn children had been placed in their hands like a bunch of clotted black grapes." (Dovey's story in Peter Balakian's family memoir, *Black Dog of Fate*)

When they reached a small village, the Armenians were fed boiled wheat.

After another long trek, they reached Mesopotamia, where there were a few water taps but no food. On the second day of their arrival, they were fed green, mildewed bread and were then locked into stables where, eventually, some of the starving went mad, after trying to find undigested kernels in animal excrement. Of the hundreds of women, only thirty survived this episode.

It was in Mesopotamia that my father lost his mother.

The circumstances, as were most in his memory, were vague.

He remembers sleeping with his mother and sister, Rose, in a graveyard. Disturbed in the middle of the night by the sound of his mother's heavy, laboured breathing, he ran to fetch something for her to drink, but when he returned, she was gone.

He surmises that she died and–as was the custom with the Turks who feared an outbreak of cholera with hundreds of corpses about them–was carried off to be dumped into a gorge.

He sees his first naked women
bent double in shame
sucked out of frayed clothes
by the sun and rampaging Turks.
Mad women with thin black lips
jump into shallow wells
full of ghostly secrets
while others watch and wait

then rush to lick their dampness
thirsty for more madness.
He lifts a small stone from ignited sand
to see if it hides water
then lets it fall
where it has always been a stone.
The sky is glutted with silence.

At some point, under circumstances shrouded by mystery, he, Rose, and their cousins, Dikran and Bedros, found refuge in an orphanage, run by Armenian administrators, with a Russian doctor on the premises, but funded and rationed by the British, and built to house twenty-five girls on an upper floor and fifty boys downstairs. Each orphan had a brass number. My father's was 75.

Rations consisted of one small loaf of bread and rice gruel in the morning. After an hour of vigorous exercise, the orphans were ravaged with hunger. They were then served a mug of black tea. In the evening came a bowl of soup with thin scraps of meat, but no more bread.

This was the orphanage visited, he claimed, by T.E. Lawrence. I have not been able to verify whether Lawrence ever mentioned such a visit. However, does this mean that I must create doubts about my father's story? Lawrence, he recalled, was a fair man with ginger hair. My father claimed to have sung for him.

Which Lawrence did he remember or think he was remembering? Was it the Lawrence of documented fact? Or David Lean's tall film hero as played with romantic fatalism by Peter O'Toole? Or a real man, unnamed to him at the time, for whom he found a name after reading history and biography?

Or did he ever, in fact, sing for anyone in the camp? Was it simply a romantic exaggeration, something to force his childish innocence out of the margin of destruction and into the center of a world that could have had him any way it pleased?

To live in the future was it necessary to invent something in the past?

Let me ask you to risk truth on the back of brief fiction.

"Armenia is a ghost, or perhaps more aptly a skeleton in the Turkish cupboard. It is a body whose flesh was long since picked clean." A sentence by David Hotham, a former correspondent in Ankara, who writes of Turkish history very much in the shadow of Kemalism, and who zealously reiterates Mustafa Kemal's pieties about "civilization": "Civilization is so strong a fire that he who ignores it is burnt and destroyed...We shall be civilized and proud of it." Hotham finds Kemal "an attractive dictator, as dictators go," for he was "the timely giant who stepped into the anarchic flux at the end of the first world war and literally changed the fate of Turkey."

In Istanbul and other large Turkish cities today there is a stock of bronze Ataturks, with fatuous *dicta* carved on plinths: "One Turk is worth a world." "I am happy to be a Turk." A plethora of petrifying memorabilia.

In his vivid travel memoir, *Anatolian Suite*, Kildare Dobbs asks a Turkish soldier what was so special about Ataturk and receives this explanation: "First he was Ghazi, always victorious. He saved our country from foreign occupation. And then he started us on the path to civilization."

The remark is incriminating. If Ataturk had, indeed, started Turks on the path to civilization, this could only mean that they were sorely lacking civilization prior to his formulaic Kemalism.

Civilization is incompatible with the slaughterhouse mentality. In Ottoman times it was left to the Greek, Armenian, and Jew to nurture and build the commercial and technical life of the empire, while the Turk sharpened his scimitar and wound his bow. "I am a Turk, and your enemy, even if I were the last man on earth." What a rallying cry for a people who want to be thought civilized!

The fiftieth anniversary of the U.N. Genocide Convention brought to mind important facts. More than a million Armenians were exterminated through direct killing, starvation, torture, and enforced death marches. Another million escaped death by fleeing into permanent exile.

When Raphael Lemkin coined the word "genocide" in 1944, he cited the 1915 slaughter of the Armenians as a seminal example of the term. This genocide is documented by Ottoman court-martial records and by thousands of documents in various international archives, in addition to eyewitness reports of missionaries and diplomats.

Yet, Turkish history is in chronic denial. Books about the genocide are banned in Turkey. Turkish guidebooks do not mention the word "Armenian," even when describing ancient or Christian artifacts and monuments. Turkish diplomats, politicians, and historians euphemistically refer to the genocide as "an unfortunate incident." *Do not believe what you hear*, the Turkish version says with equanimity.

Don't you see naked Armenian children frolicking in the water trough outside the Constantinople orphanage? There is no holocaust. The picture is not a fabrication.

But the children are alive with instinct. When they are let out of bewildering shadows of their dormitory, they simply turn joyous with play. Each carelessly scattered drop a wasted memory of what was denied them in the desert.

For a moment sadness is forgotten, as is the power of those who have made them forfeit most of childhood.

For a moment their bodies remember only pleasure.

At night when they huddle close to one another, they will remember the clay floors and clean carpets, divans covered with rugs, thick, dark fabrics, the furniture with heavy carvings, the cut flowers in flat dishes, small photographs, the religious icons–all lost in the jumbled flight.

Some will remember the nasal twangings of the *tar*, the Armenian guitar, or the airy music of the flute.

Others will remember the cakes, honey-fingers, sweet cheese biscuits, sugared fruit and melon slices, buttered *lavash* with honey, and fresh milk.

And they will all remember their mothers' gentle breath against their backs.

This is when love will cry out with particular yearning.

He and his companions were given a yearly provision of a woollen green coat, fully buttoned, two khaki shirts and trousers, stockings, and a pair of shoes. My father wore the shoes only on special occasions, preferring to roam around barefooted in order to save on leather.

At some point, he was separated from his surviving sister who disappeared. He saw her again only a few years later when the British occupied Iraq and collected orphaned children off the street.

At the age of fourteen, my father, in the company of six other boys, tried to run away from the orphanage in order to make their way to North America. They had not wanted to go to Jerusalem, the destination selected by the British, so they begged a boatman to conduct them to Basra, where they knocked at the door of an Armenian church. Given refuge in a big house with a compound, they were fed soup with rice and ordered to sleep on the ground.

This adolescence was lean, hungry, and purposeful. My father became a wage-earner, working for a childless Iraqi Christian couple who taught him Arabic. My father's duty was to take the husband his daily lunch at a salary of less than a dollar a month. Next door to the couple was an Indian customs officer who was in love with his housekeeper's daughter. He employed my father for double the money.

The British re-entered his life. He became a waiter for the RAF stationed thirty miles from Basra. This is where he learned his English, the job lasting a year before he acquired a similar job in a Basra hospital. The British wanted a waiter in Abadan and were offering good pay. He was hired, given a British passport, and spent a year and a half serving at the tables of engineers and officers. His ambition grew. After telling the Chief Engineer that he wanted to be a car mechanic, he was granted his wish. But malaria struck, eight months later, causing him to suffer from a terrible ague exactly at noon each day, and a high fever at four, before his clockwork recovery thereafter. This lasted three months. Thin and haggard after his daily diet of a single watermelon slice, he found his savings quickly depleted. But lured into a game of baccarat, he was blessed by Lady Luck and won almost thirty-five dollars. It was a time for a grand gesture: he spent a large amount of his fortune by hosting dinner for his friends at the Iraq Palace Hotel.

This was the last of his memories of Iraq and the prologue to his entry into India.

What took him to India was not the promise of spices and jewels. It had nothing to do with Oriental romance but everything to do with a desire to be reunited with his sister, Rose. Married and settled with her children in Bombay, she had sought him out through church ministers in Iraq and sent him a letter in 1927, inviting him to immigrate to India. She wanted him to be part of her new life, and she promised him a place in her home. He met her husband, Arthur Gomes, a cargo supervisor aboard a ship, two years later when Gomes visited Iraq. On the brother-in-law's second visit, in 1930, my father decided to make the journey that restored him to a part of his precious past.

India was an exaggeration from the first. His sister had conjured up visions of spacious luxury, but she and her family lived in a one-room flat in a crowded tenement. My father did not take well to the food, customs, or way of life. The chronic alien determinedly put himself outside the Indian way of life.

I know little of his bachelor years apart from his friendship with fellow-bachelors and his romantic attachment to the sister of Mervyn Grubert, who had been a P.O.W. in Burma during the British era, and who later horrified me in my boyhood with tales of Japanese eating the fried ears of prisoners.

My father had a roommate, but even he is anonymous. I am told that the two would go over to the Alimos' residence in Parel after my father had eventually met my mother, through the mediation of his friends Harry and Thelma Pascoe. He would take her and her older sister, Patsy, to the movies, and he and his roommate would play bridge with the Alimos, my father partnering Patsy, and his roommate my grandfather. My father used to annoy everyone by his smoking, and Patsy would wave him away from the card-table, as she puffed blithely on her own cigarette. He seemed down-to-earth and had a good sense of humour, even though he was given to repetition. He liked to drink, but my mother never complained about this or his clumsy dancing which was more like a walk across the floor, with a little wiggle thrown in for good measure.

Despite his friendliness, he was not, after all, Anglo-Indian. His otherness became a sticking point with her family, especially her parents. She contrived to meet him surreptitiously, turning carefully to Patsy at mass one day and whispering that she was going to see him, then slipping out of church before anyone else could notice.

Given the opposition of her parents, my father was once again a foreigner. And he was now once more in danger of losing something precious. Fortunately, my grandfather, Ewart Alimo, played diplomat, consulting his wife and his brothers to decide whether they should risk my mother's future on this strange outsider.

They knew nothing about his history or people. He could offer them little that would fill the gaps, beyond fragments of his past that proved he had stood at a place of great evil and survived. He had a strange, unsettling accent, and a will that presaged a battering force, but he also showed a warm and generous amity. They also suspected that he would tempt my mother into an elopement, and it was far better for the Alimos to have him inside their family than lose my mother to his resoluteness and unknown Armenian ways.

When I muse on this portion of my parents' story, I am struck by the odd irony of one group of historic outsiders debating the acceptance of another historic outsider.

A larger irony is surely the subtle leakage of one history into another, both extravagant in a subcontinent of exotic improbabilities.

The founder of Armenia is said in one legend to have been Hayk, the grandson of Japhet, son of Noah. There is a variant version that offers Haik as the nation's patriarch, a great archer who slew the titan Bel in an epic battle beside Lake Van. Those are the legendary versions. Legends have a way of being imprecise, even ambiguous. Hayk, Haay, Hayastan–all these names form a cluster that appears to originate from the name of the ancient kingdom of Hayasa (*c.* 1400 B.C.), situated on the eastern frontiers of the Hittite empire.

It is possible, historians suggest, that the Armenians, like the Persians and the Medes, were a subject people who had staged a *coup* against their former masters. The Hayasan language was related to several ancient Indo-European languages of Asia Minor, including Hittite, Luvian, Lydian, Lycian, and Phrygian. After the fall of the Hittite empire, the name "Hayasa" disappeared from historical records and was not found either in Assyrian or Urartian inscriptions.

The first recorded mention of the name Armenia is probably in a Persian inscription by Darius the Great. Darius inscribed on a rock face hundreds of feet above the ancient road to Babylon the names of nine nations that had revolted against him: Persia, Susa, Media, Assyria, Arminaiya, Parthia, Margiana, Sattagidia, and Sacia. Most of these are forgotten names, and the inclusion of Armenia among them gives my father's people a truly antique quality. But the history is deep and flows in various directions. Armenians appear to have been everywhere, from the Euphrates to Lake Van, the Mediterranean, the Indian Ocean, the Arabian Sea, and they made neighbours to a vast number of peoples: Phrygians, Greeks, Persians, Syrians, et cetera. Peoples who, apart from the Greeks and Persians, are as alien to me as the Armenian tongue.

There were many royal houses in their history: the royal houses of Orontes, Artaxias, Arsaces, Bagratids, Ruben (Armeno-Cilicia). The history spans over four thousand years, and the kings gave their names to major cities, enabling historians to precisely date the foundation of several key Armenian towns.

But they were mainly mountain people, hardy, vigorous, skilled, and especially good with horses and soldiery. Because they were mountain people, they could literally look down upon other peoples in the lowlands.

Armenians have a connection to the Urartians–another vague name from the distant past–and so to a civilization of towns and fortresses, agricultural and commercial fortunes. The name Urartian is a derivation from Urarat or Ararat. It conjures up images of pottery, war chariots, armour, and churning dust.

Armenian history can be read as one of wave upon wave of invasion and ethnic mingling. It can also be read as a chronicle of geographical imperatives.

Armenia was always a country cut off from the sea. To its north lay the Great Caucasian range. On the north-western side Armenia was cut off from the Black Sea by the Pontic Alps and densely wooded slopes of Lazistan. On the eastern side, it found its way to the Caspian Sea blocked by Azerbaijan. And to the south, there were the Kurds.

No wonder there were earthquakes. The land had strange fits.

Even without the earthquakes, the country was difficult. Over the exposed plains of Erzurum, Kars, and Ardahan, winter winds roared like Stentor and snow refused to melt for seven months. When temperatures fell to cruel sub-zero levels, minus forty degrees, peasants had to burrow underground.

Underground. A strange connotation. It can bring you closer to hell.

Armenia, like Russia, has trapped many generals in its savage winter throes. Lucullus was caught in 68 B.C. A seventeenth century Turkish general and his army had to turn back from Yerevan. And as recently as 1914-15, Enver Pasha was defeated, less by the Russian army than by the cruel Armenian highlands.

Such cold makes for great legends. When asked by a traveller whether there was any summer in Erzerum, a dervish replied:

> By God, I remained there eleven months and nine and twenty days, the people said that summer was coming, but I did not see it. It happened, however, that a cat, which ran over the roofs of the houses, became frozen there while in the act of running, and remained so for the space of nine months, when the spring arriving, the cat began to thaw, cried 'Miau!' and fell down.

The last king of Armenia was Leon VI who, within a few months of his coronation, was besieged by an army of over thirty thousand Mamelukes. That was the end of the Armenian kingdom and of official Christianity. Leon languished for seven years in a royal prison, which allowed him ample time to perfect the arts of calligraphy and petition-writing. Later, as an exile in France, he taught King Charles VI how to play chess. He went on to further fame in England when he delivered to King Richard II and the English Parliament a proposal to end the Hundred Years' War. Although the Archbishop of Canterbury successfully rejected Leon's plea for peace, Richard rewarded the Armenian king with a considerable pension.

He died in France and was laid to rest in the Church of the Celestins with pomp and ceremony. His funeral was attended by many princes and lords, and his monument was in the company of those of French monarchs.

Like most Armenians, he died an exile, a part of someone else's story.

We can all be part of someone else's story. I see an Atom Egoyan film that is set in Armenia and I find myself a little in the central character, find myself a part of his discourse, find myself watching him observing Armenian history.

Atom, surely a pun on Adam, but with nuclear energy packed into an infinitesimal unit of chemical individuality, ready to mushroom, just like the consequences of the first man made from the ground. Egoyan, Ego film art, but really less ego and more art. Metacinema of a cold, subtle inspiration. An expatriate Egyptian Armenian. We are all exiles, with a problem of communication, a repetitive compulsion, a narrative swallowing itself like Uroborus in an attempt at mandalic wholeness. But it's not the plot that matters. It's the icons of pain, radiant among the chronic confusions and surface textures. Emblems of misunderstanding, interrupted sequences, montages of depression.

I viewed *Calendar* one evening to find traces of Armenia, and I did in nuanced images. Layers and layers folded upon one another. The overt story is one of love lost, how a North American Armenian filmmaker loses his beloved, a professional translator and also Armenian, to their driver-guide in Armenia, while he is visiting the country to photograph old churches for calendar art. There is the acute irony of an unsuspected affair occurring in translation, and the poignant melancholy of the woman walking across a frame and disappearing with her new lover as the filmmaker keeps his focus on the old church, his professional motive for coming to Armenia in the first place.

But the reverberations are almost endless, the teasing suggestions, imagination's companions. Is the guide an emblem of the country and language the filmmaker has lost and cannot understand except in snippets of translation by his beloved? And are the objects he photographs emblems of time lost, time remembered, time redeemed, or time misunderstood? He is nominally Armenian and has sponsored a young female Armenian foster child, but he is cut off from Armenia by his attitudes, adopted language, cold concentration on technical matters about video, film, message machines, scripts, and letters. He is outside the country, outside the churches he is filming. Beyond his love affair, he shows no sentimentality, and worries only about his budget, the lighting, and whether he owes the talkative guide more than he'd bargained for. Knowing no Armenian and little or no history, he does not enter into a dialogue with the guide, and is not even able to express what it means when he hears his beloved's translation of the guide's stories.

But there is a covert story that infiltrates almost every image, a very Armenian story that flashes by sometimes as a pale image of mighty Ararat glimpsed from a window, or of sheep crowding a rural road. Armenia, with its antique history, makes his beloved forget their own history of love. She is ready to be assimilated by Armenia. He remains fractured from the country and its identity, unable in Canada to find any woman who can share more than a bottle of red wine and music for a brief dinner with him. The women come and go, and they are of different backgrounds–Macedonian, Italian, Russian, Egyptian, Indian–perhaps emblematic of the countries and civilizations that absorbed exiled Armenians at various stages in history. So, the filmmaker remains isolated in his suffering.

This film, with its recurring visual refrains and recursive themes, moves me in a subtle, underwater way.

To flute song and drum a pastoral
beginning on the mountain road
an unending flock of sheep coarse
tufted carry us along to a sad story
about churches and calendars.
There is an energy in each place
that goes beyond beauty.
Nothing is accidental: the sky
and the church refuse chance.

A cluster of brown turrets asks:
What does it mean when you hear our story?
And stones pocked by centuries are a mute chorus.
Come closer, stranger. Touch

and feel how we are constructed
well composed, naturally lit, seductive.
It's all a matter of watching
letting your eye discover the already
without a translator.
These places make him feel a stranger
remind him he has forgotten
ancestral dreams.
[He is] *from here, but being here has made* [him]
from somewhere else.
What is the best image for what he knows,
and will it be significant rocks and cliffs
and turrets and the people who made that history?
A church and fortress in ruins release his musing:
*"All that is meant to protect us is bound to fall
apart, bound to become contrived, useless and absurd.
All that's meant to protect is bound to isolate, and
all that's meant to isolate is bound to hurt."*

I can't get my own tongue around most of the names: Movses Khorenatsi, Agathangelos, Eghishe, John Mamikonian, Grigor Narekats'i, Aristakes of Lastivert, Asoghik of Taron, Prince Gregory Majistros, Stepan Orbelian, Prince Hethum, the Katholicos Nerses Shnorhali. My tongue trips over the syllables even as I sense the vibrations set off by these revered names of Armenian historians, scholars, seer-poets, itinerant teachers. I am unfamiliar with all of them and all of their works, yet I sense the pride my father's people feel in their contributions to his dispersed culture. It is similar to the pride I feel when I unexpectedly meet an Armenian in Mississauga, Toronto, Guelph, Cambridge, Kitchener, Windsor, or Stoney Creek. I am grateful that they have survived history's amnesia.

My father's knowledge of Armenian myths would dwindle today beside my acquired information of the same.

He never mentioned to any of us the myth of Queen Semiramis of Assyria who is reputed to have fallen in love with the Armenian prince, Ara the Fair. According to the myth, Semiramis invaded Armenia to impress Ara with her power. But he selected to be killed in battle rather than yield to her desires. Despairing, she left the fertile valley of Araxes and retreated south. Arriving at the eastern shore of a great salt lake (now familiarly known as Lake Van), she saw a high rocky hill rising above streams of fresh water and flourishing villages. Here, with the help of 12,000 workmen and 6,000 skilled craftsmen from Assyria, she built a magnificent city, surrounded by strong walls with bronze gates. (Armenians were extraordinary metal-smiths) She also built herself a royal palace on a lofty crag, grander than any other edifice in existence.

We can follow her story in a chronicle of Armenia by the fifth century A.D. Armenian historian, Moses of Khoren (Movses Khorenats'i):

> The whole city was girt with immense walls for its protection. Now, the eastern side of the mountain had such a hard surface that even an iron-pointed stylo could not impress a single line upon it; yet, palaces, long galleries and strong-rooms for the queen's treasure were hewn out of its side.

However, no one, apart from her retinue, was allowed in. Entrances to the queen's temples and apartments bore inscriptions carved in solid rock. No one could read or decipher the inscriptions because they were in a secret script.

That is the myth. The historical reality is different. There is no evidence that Semiramis invaded Armenia or that she attempted to make love to King Arame (Ara).

The myth forces us to read between history's lines. It tells us a story of black romanticism. Semiramis' tale is a tale about lust, invasion, conquest, and humiliation. It is grand in the vein of grand desolation. The Armenians are forced to be part of someone else's story once again. And at the end of it, they are deprived of a meaning.

Occasionally history and myth converge. However, my father would never have known Sir John Maundeville's account of Erzeroum, the great city cruelly wasted by the Turks: "Thereabout groweth no Wine nor Fruit, or else little or none. In this Land is the Earth more high than in any other and that maketh great Cold. And there be many good Waters and good Wells that come under Earth from the River of Paradise, that is clept Euphrates, that is a Day's Journey from the City."

And certainly I have no record of my father's ever knowing the interesting legend, recorded by the same Maundeville, of the Lady and the Sparrow-Hawk:

> In that country is an old castle that stands upon a rock, which is called the Castle of the Sparrow-Hawk, beyond the city of Layays, which belongeth to the rich Lordship of Cruk, a good, Christian man; where a 'Fair Lady of Faerie' keeps a sparrow-hawk upon a perch. 'And who that will watch that sparrow-hawk seven days and seven nights, without company and without sleep, that fair Lady shall give him his first earthly wish. And one time it befell that a King of Armenia, that was a worthy knight and doughty man, and a noble prince, watched that Hawk for seven days and seven nights, and the Lady came to him and bade him wish, for he had well deserved it. And he answered that he was a great Lord enough, and well in Peace, and had enough of worldly Riches; and therefore he would wish none other Thing, but the Body of that fair Lady, and to have it at his Will. And she answered him, that he knew not what he asked, for she said that he should not ask but an earthly Thing, for she was none earthly Thing but a ghostly Thing....'But since that I may not withdraw you from your lewd Courage, I shall

> give you without Wishing, and to all them that shall come of your Lineage, Sir King! ye shall have War without Peace, and always to the 9th Generation ye shall be in Subjection of your Enemies, and ye shall be in Need of all Goods.' And since then, neither that King of Armenia nor the Country were ever in Peace; neither had they ever since then Plenty of Goods; and they have been since then always under Tribute to the Saracens.

The message is undeniable even beneath the elegant folds of fourteenth century rhetoric. This is an ancient curse that is too well borne out by modern history.

The hot sands are a still universe until a wind comes up suddenly, creating blowing veils of dust, ridges of dry rigour. Conversation is impossible; the furnace of air will blowtorch their throats. If they look up from the imprints of sand beneath their feet, they see only more brown or ochre, a voiceless expanse set off by a blue sky out of which death could drop like a sudden slice of a sword.

Their eyes are forced downwards to their feet sinking in sand, but they don't really sink, not the way they would in quicksand. Here, the sand does not shake underfoot. It is a brown screen for their quivering shadows.

The desert is not a romantic presence.

The hours fall like dead flies. They have only trudged a few miles, and already the sky is a shuddery blue. It is beginning to unnerve them.

If there were food and drink available, they would all have the spontaneous savagery of the starved.

There is no diagram for their journey. There are no maps. The desert has the same layout for miles.

He knows nothing about blueprints which assure us that nothing surprising will ever happen.

Here, there are no places for people.

The caravan of urchins makes its ghostly way, experiencing only expected afflictions.

He remembers how water tasted in his homeland
The desert has only an illusion of water
a ghost of plenty.
Thirst makes him guilty
He wishes he hadn't been so wasteful
splashing it about him
watching it form puddles at his feet
or snake in the dust
becoming as narrow as a thief
slipping through cracks in a doorway.
Even if they bring him stale water
brown with tadpoles
he will drink,
pretending it is a disguise–
the darkness of water before creation–
like the drops turning to snow near Ararat.

He will even drink mouthfuls
from the Kemakh gorge,
his lips red with the taste
of bodies flung to the end of the world.

They are crossing invisible borders of life and death, moving into strange lands, conscious and alone beside one another in pain, fear, and trembling. In the solitude of sleep, imagined horrors multiply: where in the territory of earth are they now?

Cries for a little water, whimpers of fatigue are the only verbal exchanges, as they anticipate only more landscape.

There is nothing to do but improvise, though they don't know the word. Their minds move on silence.

On torn and swelling feet, they remember everything they see and where they saw it last, especially food, water, women, and Turks.

Some scurry up to the front leaders of the march once or twice to see how much longer this will last.

Saliva takes the place of fresh water, but they don't swallow in one gulp. There isn't enough for that.

They dream dreams and interpret them during the day. There is time enough for that.

Dreams are a strange language that are created on Ararat, far above the blood-red poppies, and then blown into their sleep across the sand dunes.

Waking is full of blanks which are filled as they await the arrival of more landscape.

What are the words which genocide demands? Are words for the gratification of the writer alone, or are they meant to advertise the horror? Should I simply speak the facts and step aside, allowing what is so slippery to promote my desire to be sensitive? Take these words as a supplement to what my father remembers. Take these words as a supplement to myself.

It just keeps happening over and over. The violence of sore feet, enforced marching, dry throats. And the repentance for any minor sin that has brought on the violence.

The truth is this: the violence is real; the repentance unnecessary.

But the distinction is alien to his juvenescent mind that knows only the violence and the repentance.

"Let this pain pass from me. I will be good."

But it just keeps happening over and over.

There is no plot in his story. Nor is there a construction of any sort, apart from cruelty and distress. He is uncertain of the motive.

His young life moves in a series of halts and marches. There is no hero or heroine to save him.

He is too young for absolute truth, and nobody is uttering an explanation that he could possibly understand.

By June, 1915, as the Russians made incursions into Turkish territory with the help of Armenian contingents, the Turks multiplied their atrocities. The Vali Djevdet Bey destroyed entire Armenian villages, sparing neither men, women, nor children. Elsewhere, at Siirt, a general massacre occurred on June 17, and was reported by a young Venezuelan soldier who was serving with the Turkish armed forces:

> Fathers, brothers, sons, and grandsons lay there as they had fallen beneath the bullets and *yataghans* of the assassins. From more than one slashed throat the life gushed forth in mouthfuls of warm blood. Flocks of vultures were perched upon the mound, pecking at the eyes of the dead and dying, whose rigid gaze seemed still to mirror the horrors of unspeakable agony; while the scavenger dogs struck sharp teeth into the entrails of beings still palpitating with the breath of life.

Soon afterwards, this same teenaged soldier came upon a caravan of several hundred women and children, resting in a village marketplace:

Their sunken cheeks and cavernous eyes bore the stamp of death. Among the women, almost all of whom were young, were some mothers with children, or, rather, childish skeletons, in their arms. One of them was mad. She knelt beside the half-putrefied cadaver of a new-born babe. Another woman had fallen to the ground, rigid and lifeless. Her two little girls, believing her asleep, sobbed convulsively as they tried in vain to awaken her. By her side, dying in a scarlet pool, was yet another, beautiful and very young, the victim of a soldier of the escort. The velvety eyes of the dying girl, who bore every evidence of refinement, mirrored an immense and indescribable agony....

They should have been buried in ice or peat:
the spirit would remember the body perfectly–
how this woman once called to her son
while stuffing vine leaves with nuts and rice
how this girl flashed eyes at this boy
(her neck slashed, his right arm sundered)
how this old man prayed
while flames ate his flesh in the church pyre
how this mother, with the bayonet plugging her
vulva,
would have loved this baby in her belly
calling his name to the stars
dancing in the night sky
how this child, newly born, its brains splattering
rock
would have loved Beethoven
imagining a moonlight sonata.
Their memories could have been revelations,
their passions a validation of ambition.

Their murders are a statistic, not a metaphor,
though their spirits are encoded in air
currents and river sediment.

Up to their knees in death, the Turks go on
killing with an insistence on being perfect.
Each slaughter is prefaced with prayer–
fanatacism is a pristine religion.
They see the sweet salt blood
running all the way to Damascus
and they laugh in ecstasy
at pyramids of flesh
covering bone-pits sad jewels of the dead.
Under the Euphrates
are minarets of skulls
filigreed with last thoughts
into which fishes glide.
From Angora to Zeitun, A to Z of sudden history,
generations vanish in a wilderness
blinded by locust wings.
For those who survive
it is the end of cosmos:
they are absurd heroes
rewarded with nightmares
of how easily we are overcome
how cleverly destroyed.

My father's story can be complemented by thousands of accounts by other survivors, but very few of these have ever seen print in English and in a readable form. One book, however, that does convey a clear idea of what my father survived is Kerop Bedoukian's *The Urchin*. This memoir begins pastorally, with remembrances of courtyards, fruit gardens, milch cows, and lambs. The Bedoukian household numbers about twenty, ranging from a baby to grandmother Mariam who is paralyzed on one side but who chain-smokes, sometimes with a little *hashish* added. But the pastoral mood is superficial, for the "body-odour" of race reeks in the air. In Sivas, even the watchdogs of the Armenians and Turks smell of race; in Aleppo, even the orphans, who look like expressionless, neglected, lethargic zombies, are unsafe as the Turks spread like a red death through the streets, hunting for victims. Some children know their names and a few give Turkish counterparts. Half of them know where they are born but none know the date.

The author's family begins to come apart. His soldier-father, like my paternal grandfather, is incaracerated and then never heard from again. Kerop's elder brother disguises himself as a female but eventually has to abandon this masquerade and face certain extinction. His youngest sister perishes, but his sturdy mother does not pause to mourn. "Leave the dead and take care of the living." It is easy to isolate this event and magnify the heroism extravagantly, but Kerop Bedoukian resists the opportunity because even such almost hallucinatory courage is a small detail in a larger design of struggle and freedom. The Turkish gendarmes, who take target practice on Armenian women, do not give anyone time to grieve. Everyone is running. Everyone is looking for a way to live to see another sunrise.

A mile away from the caravan of urchins and elders is the Euphrates river, but the water cannot be reached. The Turkish soldiers watch as the marchers fall prey to villagers or tribesmen who raid the group and scavenge for gold, animals, and females who can serve as slaves or concubines. Young girls are raped and commit suicide, mothers die of starvation or broken hearts, some of the living go mad. The Armenians cannot prevent their suffering from becoming a spectacle. They are not even allowed to defecate in peace, for the Turks go around beating excrement with sticks in order to find gold pieces or ornaments that might once have been swallowed furtively.

The young Kerop has a naif curiosity and sense of adventure in the midst of all the atrocities. He enjoys playing the hero in his own romancings and in fact. He repulses a youthful Turk in Birejik who tries to woo his eldest sister; he narrowly escapes an axe-wielding Kurd; much later, after the massacres and war are over, he dives into the water of a harbour to retrieve valuable papers for his sisters.

It is this way of adventuring and dreaming that converts the story from a mere record of death and destruction to a testament of will-power and achievement. At twelve, he becomes the eldest surviving male in his family, but he is blessed with a strong mother who is as resourceful as she is determined to get the best deal she can for her dependents. Her faith in God is as indomitable as her will and ingenuity. She obtains money by pretending to be related to a wealthy dead woman. She is an expert weaver. And she holds the shrinking family together in Constantinople where the Armenians are protected by the intervention of European embassies.

The Urchin comes to a sense of closure as Kerop starts a new life in North America. He goes on to serve for twenty years as President of the Montreal chapter of the Armenian General Benevolent Union. He helps thousands of Armenians emigrate from Turkey, Greece, and Egypt to Canada. In 1967 the Canadian government honours his humanitarianism by granting him the Centennial Medal. His survival is a repudiation of human brutality and the obscenity of history.

In David Kherdian's novel about his own mother's life, *The Road From Home*, the unshakable grandmother claims: "However we may be dispersed, we are one family. If one of us should die, something in all of us will die, and if only one of us lives, then some part of each of us will live."

Sometimes we feel guilty for deserting our hate, but how, as a Jewish survivor of the Nazi holocaust once asked rhetorically, can we live despising the world?

We sometimes survive by dreams.

Turkish denial of Armenian history, reality, and extermination is a devil's reproach. The Armenian writer Gostan Zarian recorded in his diary at the end of the summer of 1922: "There is horrible misery on the shores of the Bosphorus. In the streets, fragments of humanity with terror in their eyes. Sinister glances from Turks.

Whispered talk....Our loss is so enormous that it is impossible to write about it....It is not easy being an Armenian. Perhaps it is our function to illuminate some dark corner of the universe."

Peter Balakian's perceptive scholar-aunt observes in *Black Dog of Fate*: "Because territory has eluded us, we have a freedom to invent that most people don't. The more our geography shrinks, the more our imaginations expand, the more we're like owls flying in the dark."

With their dying, I am my parents' guardian. Of history–or of such fragments as I can recall. My mother, I know, would not have concerned herself with such possession, retention, and articulation. Although a sentimentalist, she could sometimes be careless about what she preserved of the past. Consequently, I have few family photographs or letters.

My father was a hoarder. Of Armenian church bulletins with their incessant appeals for donations. Of magazines on mechanics. Of two or three Armenian novels and histories. Old ties, socks, shoes, and suits were stuffed in drawers, cupboards, and on shelves. Psychically possessed by the phobia of dispossession, he collected things as if they could be put to use in some far-off time.

"A junk-collector," my mother would complain. "A real *jerry-prana*!" The Hindi word relegated him to the level of Indian rag-and-bone men.

But he knew all about disappearance.

NAKED ADAM

My father was, in certain ways, a primitive. His passions lay deep but when they surfaced it was in the form of violent eruptions. He was the best of friends and the worst of enemies. Loyalty was a key virtue in him and because he remained loyal to weaker men, he expected reciprocal loyalty from them. Sometimes he refused to acknowledge their character flaws, and this would frustrate my mother who accused him of trusting these hangers-on more than he trusted some of his own relatives.

He had a temper that could quickly degenerate into violence. He was easily provoked by miscalculating neighbours, and when he was a younger man he had once almost killed a blasphemous Muslim who had persisted in defying him. Taking offence at something the man had said, he seized him by the neck, rushed him to a nearby tank of water and held his head underwater until a burly Pathan intervened.

A more terrifying incident was one that I personally witnessed when I was a mere boy. Theresa, my much older cousin, had surprised us one evening by an unexpected visit with the young man she had just married. They had met in a sanatorium where they were both recuperating from respiratory problems. What should have been an occasion for joyful celebration abruptly turned dangerous. Theresa's young man was a Jew and therefore *odar,* a foreigner or outsider, in the Armenian scheme of things.

My father, who was well on his way to inebriation in the company of friends, was enraged. Grabbing what in my memory was a kitchen knife, he stalked the couple around a table before he was physically restrained by some of his male friends. The episode was brief, loud, and traumatic. It troubled me unceasingly.

What had generated such irrational behaviour? Was it Sam's Jewishness? The fact that he was *odar*? For years I was unsure, and for years I was ashamed of my father. He had never betrayed any anti-Semitism earlier, obviously aware of the close parallels between Jewish and Armenian history. Resentment, persecution, dispersion, genocide. These were common to both Jew and Armenian. He also had Jewish colleagues and neighbours.

Was he merely reacting viscerally to Theresa's betrayal of her Armenian roots? Hardly. Theresa was only half-Armenian: Rose's daughter, she also belonged to her dysfunctional Goan father. My father himself was in a way less than fully Armenian because he could remember only fragments of his own ancestors and country. Perhaps, this was it: the fear of becoming even more fragmented.

When I returned to this incident many decades later during a conversation with my mother, I learned that what had propelled my father's fury was a sense of a different betrayal. A child of massacre, he had had a dark legacy which he only partially understood and managed, passing it along to his children through his genes. His love and family feeling were real but crude. He was not obsessive about outsiders–he had, after all, married one himself, and he was an outsider in India–but he did have a zealous craving for dignity and a pathological respect for what had been or what might come.

"He wanted her to ask his permission," my mother explained.

My father had been Theresa's surrogate-parent, ever mindful of her health, safety, and future after her own father decided to drown his bleary future at the bottom of a bottle.

As such, he had determined that he would survive at any means and that his blood-relatives had to live for themselves and their ancestors, retaining by instinct or instruction a will to keep the best of Armenian wisdom. And this had meant family feeling, respect for the patriarch, and an effort to keep the hearth safe and warm. "You make the house round" is an Armenian maxim. Theresa's impromptu decision to give her heart to her beloved was read by my father as an outrageous betrayal of his own yearning to keep the Armenian house round and secure.

Perhaps, my father feared that one more part of his family history would be lost with her sudden elopement. Perhaps, he had made a secret, solemn promise to his dying sister, Rose, that he would keep her children faithful to what made them undeniably Armenian, despite mixed bloodlines.

He had loved my cousin as his own child. He had loved her so much that he might attack and possibly kill another man who seemed to threaten this bond.

Despite the eventual reconciliation of my father and the two victims of his violent anger, there is no relief for my questioning.

It was an ugly, terrifying incident which I cannot disguise or exorcize. Suckled on atrocity, my father accepted violence and the shadow of death as elemental forces, and because I was his son, I, too, was forced into the dark pain.

He claimed to be Armenian Orthodox in faith and took great pride in pointing out that his people were the first to adopt Christianity as an official state religion. But he never attended any church services, except for weddings, funerals, baptisms or special occasions such as Easter and Christmas. And even then, he would walk out during the sermon to enjoy a cigarette break with other like-minded men.

He was, as his own people put it, a "holiday Christian." He liked liturgical ritual and music, especially Gregorian chants. He liked the sensuousness of ceremonies, the richly embroidered robes, the symbolic colours, the silver censers wafting incense, the prescribed bowing, genuflecting, and service of the altar boys and sacristans. He was impatient with practically everything else, mildly scoffing at church doctrine and challenging what little dogma he knew.

As he never mentioned how Armenia became a Christian nation, I doubt whether he was familiar with the myth related by Agathangelos, chronicler of national legends. Christianity had reached Armenia possibly through Bartholomew (one of the Twelve Apostles) and Thaddeus, who were the first to evangelize in Armenia. So, it can truly be said that the Armenian Church which developed from this preaching was an apostolic one. However, the actual circumstance of national conversion makes for an interesting story by Agathangelos.

This tale features King Tiridates III who was renowned for revenge, torture, and lust. This king's father had been assassinated by a younger member of a Parthian noble family, thereby instigating a blood feud between the two royal houses. Gregory, the secret assassin, was quietly removed to Cappadocia, where he converted to Christianity. Returning to Armenia, Gregory began preaching the gospel, but when Tiridates discovered his responsibility for the royal assassination, he tortured the preacher and threw him into a dungeon for fifteen years.

Tiridates descended into further cruelty. When a young girl rejected his lusty advances, he killed her and her thirty-nine companions. Then, as Agathangelos relates, he lost all contact with humanity: "the king took on the appearance of a wild boar, and dwelt among the beasts. He went to a place covered in reeds, where he munched the grass like a wild animal, and rolled in the fields entirely naked."

Tiridates' sister believed that none but the prisoner Gregory could cure him. And when Gregory was released from his dungeon and set about curing the afflicted monarch, the conversion of the entire Armenian nobility followed.

One Christian feast that my father especially liked was Easter, the miracle of the Risen Christ. In the Armenia of his ancestors, Easter season began with *Parkendagh*, a great celebration on the Tuesday before Lent, when a whole lamb was slaughtered, then grilled for *shish kebab*, accompanied by pilaf, side dishes, and rich desserts such as *loukhum* (jellied candy), *halva*, and *rojig* (grape and walnut rolls). Then Lent, the time of fasting and abstinence would begin and last forty days, with no fish or meat consumed. But at the end there would be a climactic feast, a meal to end all meals, on Easter Eve: *lahmajoon*, *bamiya*, *fassoulyah*, *enguinar*–meats and vegetables, always including onion, sometimes stewed, sometimes simply chopped or grilled–and the intriguing *imam bayeldi*, Turkish for "the priest fainted," a humorous acknowledgement of the overpowering strength of garlic and onion. Food that today can be seen as a secular mythology, a complexly encoded script that embodies what Peter Balakian calls the "long history and collective memory of our Near Eastern culture," as well as "a drama whose meaning [is] entwined in Armenia's bitter history."

Easter was a fine time for children, little girls in pink and blue dresses, boys in their best clothing. Easter was a time for family visits with the traditional greeting for the hosts at their door: "Christ is risen from the dead!" and the reply: "Blessed be the resurrection of Christ!" Then kisses for elders' hands, one by one, and then, best of all, the gifts. Coloured eggs for all, and contests where each youngster would hold an egg, with its tip just showing, in a fist, and crack down on an opponent's egg to see which one would smash right through.

What religious and cultural coding in the ceremonials! The inveterate faith in a God who cared enough to be a scapegoat and who would then escape from the tomb and reappear in full body. But which Armenian ever suspected that April would become the cruellest month, for Easter, 1915 would be a time of death and no resurrection.

My father did many noble things for friends and family, and one of the noblest was his generosity to his sister's children. When Rose died of an abscessed liver a few years after my birth, she left behind four children, two of whom were still of school age. Her husband, Arthur, nicknamed "Baldy" because of his premature baldness, allowed his thirst for booze to overwhelm his fatherly duties, and the two youngest, Stephen and Neville, were dependent on my father for food, clothing, and education, whereas the eldest children, Aubrey and Theresa, had to look to their own lives. Rose's children never forgot his generosity and concern. Sometimes they even allowed their gratitude to blind them to my father's obvious defects. They must surely have known that at times he acted upon wild instincts.

Some of my lasting impressions are of his appetites and lack of inhibition. He liked to drink and usually to immoderate excess, so that his speech quickly became slurred and incomprehensible to me. As his blood warmed to the invasion of alcohol, his argumentativeness grew fiercer, and one was often afraid of impending violence. He did not ever want to be challenged intellectually, and he certainly did not tolerate his son's audacious refusal to acquiesce in arguments.

When inebriated, he could lose other aspects of decorum as well. Once, at a picnic with friends, he cast off his bathing trunks and walked into the surf totally nude, literally a naked Adam. This exhibition brought embarrassment to his wife and children, but none to him.

That instance was another when I wished to reinvent myself as someone other than my father's son. It made me feel that to be an Armenian was somehow to be associated with embarrassment, with base instinct or indulgence.

Today, that incident assumes a different cast. It becomes a code of a different sort. What he had survived during his childhood was the ultimate nakedness, the soul-scarring humiliation of being dependent on mere vestigial humanity. After exposure to Turkish atrocity, what could possibly embarrass him about the human form? What more could he expose about himself? His manhood was simply naked flesh inappropriately uncovered. But his orphaned childhood and desert odyssey were real obscenity, uncivilized suffering caused by wholly indecent perpetrators. After having been forced to tortuous starvation, he could sometimes slip into animality himself.

PAIN AS INTIMATE AS LOVE

My mother was not an admirer of Armenian etiquette. She thought the people to be rather uncouth, their food coarse, their cooking manners unhygienic.

She was disgusted by *madzoon* (yogurt) and the method of churning butter in the membrane of a goat. She would never go anywhere near *baghsgutahn*, a curd product, or *surkik* made with dry cottage cheese. The very thought of *khavoorma*, cooked meat sealed in its own fat, made her ill. She knew that living conditions in historic Armenia had been backward and downtrodden, but little did she know about certain facts: for instance, that the vast majority of their population were peasants who lived in villages on the plains of Erzerum, Pasin, and Moush. These rough, weather-beaten people lived underground with their domesticated animals in something resembling large burrows. Light entered their rooms through oiled paper. Warmth was provided by fireplaces where dried cowdung and straw smouldered, and smoke was emitted through chimneys resembling large toadstools, rising above snow or grass, and covered by stone.

These were not dainty or genteel people; they could not afford to be so.

When survival is paramount, there is little time or occasion for soap-cleaned hands.

Michael J. Arlen reveals in his beautifully affecting book, *Passage To Ararat*, that he has always hated being an Armenian because he was given the values of Europeans who had despised the Armenians. As Arlen explains: "And I have hated my father not, as I have thought all these years, for being too strong a figure or too authoritarian but because he, so to speak, steppped back and gave me to the Europeans."

Arlen's father had changed his name from Dikran Kouyoumjian to Michael Arlen. Born in Bulgaria, he had been reared in England, educated in English schools, and was an English citizen with English codes of manner. He played tennis, socialized in English circles, rarely talked about Armenia and he almost never wrote about it. His novels were romantic in tone, with a dandyish air, and his own image was that of a cool, elegant, impassive figure. He sometimes smiled in public but rarely in private, and his sad eyes and English manner stamped him as something other than Armenian. He had a cool air of detachment, quite the opposite of excitable Armenian passion. His sophisticated English mimicry distanced him from the stereotype of the Armenian rug-merchant or peasant.

But the Englishness was a mask that slipped off the Armenian face when challenged by historical fact. England was culpable for much Armenian suffering.

The most dedicated of all the western powers to the cause of the Ottoman Turks, particularly because of Turkey's ability to prevent Russia from reaching the Mediterranean, Britain became Turkey's best commercial customer in the nineteenth century. The English Conservatives sometimes seemed to be Turkophiles, even though, in reality, their true purpose was to arm their eastern ally against their common imperial enemy, Russia. As English historian Christopher J. Walker explains in his modern history of Armenia, "three things made the Conservatives favour the Turks. All concerned prestige or money." The first was "imperial jealousy of Russia, and fear that she would either make a direct attack upon India, or impede Britain's communications with her possession." The second was a fear that large British investments in Ottoman bonds would disappear if the country itself were lost to invasion. The third was a concern for the important overland trade route to India, which brought trade to both Britain and Turkey. The English pretended to take a humane interest in the plight of the Armenians, going so far as to extract from the sultan promises to introduce necessary reforms and to protect Christian and other subjects of the Porte or sovereign Turkish government. Sadly, even Benjamin Disraeli, a Jew and as such no stranger to the issue of discrimination and persecution, did not attempt to assert strong moral values in imperial economic and political policy. Indeed, it can be credibly argued that Disraeli's indifference to Armenian suffering in Ottoman Turkey was a contributing factor to extensive Armenian oppression. The British Conservatives paid only lip service to issues of justice and humane laws; the Turks knew full well that by pretending to heed British appeals, they could fool Britain into turning her face away as the Turks then casually resumed their business of persecuting the Armenians under the guise of national unity and security.

In some ways, my father had a blind spot when it came to Britain. "An Englishman is always true to his word," he maintained, though there was ample evidence to the contrary.

He certainly was unaware of the famous *Punch* cartoon of July 20, 1878, depicting Disraeli and the Lady of Cyprus attempting to hoist a fat Turkish Humpty-Dumpty back on to the wall. Its caption read: "Humpty-Dumpty sat on a wall;/Humpty-Dumpty had a great fall; Dizzy, with Cyprus, and all the Queen's men,/Hopes to set Humpty-Dumpty up again."

My father recognized some of Britain's insidious use of colonial power in India, but he romanticized her value as a civilized nation. He spoke nostalgically of "the good old days" when there was no Prohibition and liquor could flow copiously at parties, when there was no refugee problem in Bombay, no squatters littering the streets like chronic eruptions, when pavements and buildings were clean, when clubs could hold swanky *soirées*, when Anglo-India was still the Raj rather than down-at-the-heels. He proudly boasted of his British passport as a guarantee of privileged status. He renounced it only when we immigrated to Canada after my mother decided that Blighty was not Home, after all.

The fact is that no help came from the British when it was most needed.

Turkish Armenia was to all intents and purposes a British protectorate after the Cyprus Convention, even though the region was never officially given that title. Armenians of the Ottoman Empire foolishly believed that the great powers, led by Britain, would intervene in Ottoman affairs. Britain, supposedly a fountainhead of civilized law, would surely see that the Ottoman system of law was really a denial of law itself. Muslim law was inapplicable to non-Muslims. A Muslim in confict with another Muslim was guaranteed a fair hearing in civil cases, but a non-Muslim in conflict with a Muslim always lost, because the case was heard before a religious tribunal where non-Muslim testimony was forbidden.

The English did nothing about this. They also did nothing about the fact that Armenians were prohibited from bearing arms—even in self-defence against predatory neighbours. They did nothing about the *devshirme* or boy-collection, whereby officials could seize children from the Christian communities, educate them as Muslims and press them into the Ottoman civil service. They did nothing about the poll-tax and property tax, which in practice amounted to unchecked extortion. They did nothing about the obligation to provide free winter quarters *(kishlak)* to nomadic Kurds and their flocks, often for four to six months annually.

The English adopted a stiff upper lip–as usual, but when the evidence mounted about the British government's failure to the Armenians, the Blue Books or published collections of government documents for the general public stopped appearing. The Blue Books were simply too embarrassing to the British government.

Of course, the English had their usual *bête-noire* in the Russians, and they played it for all it was politically worth. In this manner, they could hold fast to the Ottoman connection without really interfering in internal Turkish matters that embroiled the Armenians.

They had blood on their white hands, even as they slept continently at night.

Harold Bond (Bondjukian), Armenian-American poet, recalls the same story of imperial neglect in his poignant poem, "Postscript: Marash," where he cites the Turkish bloodbaths in Marash, Musa Dagh, Aintab, and Ourfa. The year his maternal uncle is beheaded, the Turks issue religious tolerance for the empire, while in England, William Watson writes his "purple sonnets for the lost/nation," thereby becoming famous. From Egypt, Cyprus, and Lebanon, the Armenian Legion fight under the command of General Allenby for a homeland, but have nothing to show years later except wrinkles over their ugly scars.

Why my father did not condemn the British is a matter I fail to understand. Perhaps, denied humanity by the Turks, he mistook English good manners for genuine benevolence, not realizing that these manners had nothing to do with particular interest in him or with Indians in general. English manners in England or in the colonies bear no relation to actual attitudes, for as Germaine Greer has remarked, the Englishman is "uniformly polite to everyone," and, so, his manners "are totally insincere."

Perhaps there was another reason for my father's delusion.

Perhaps humiliation and suffering finally subjugate a victim into misreading grand historical gestures. The British were famous for grand historical gestures, even when these followed centuries of racial intolerance, bigotry, oppression, and repression. The Raj came to an inglorious end, but the English preserved a sense of panoplied dignity, a sense of occasion by dressing up Mountbatten in all his pristine regalia and officiating with pomp and ceremony as the sun set on their long rule in India.

My father memorialized their leave-taking with nostalgic fondness, quite oblivious to the fact that there was (as Paul Scott came to feel and express in *The Raj Quartet*) something unctuous and evasive about the way the British left. They had been careless in their division of the spoils: India had been badly fractured into rival sects, the princes abandoned to nationalist revenge, the Anglo-Indians left to twice-born contempt. The Quit India Movement had spawned bloody savagery. My grandmother's second husband, an unrepentant Englishman named Ken Face who used to dress in khaki shirt, short trousers, and stockings, had had his skull cracked by hooligans in Bombay. And yet, even after all this turmoil and violence, the British had left an undying legacy of racial discrimination. In 1945 it was quite impossible for a British officer to mix with Indian civilians on equal terms; in 1964 (three years after we left India) there were still beach bungalows at Juhu where the English could drink liquor with the tacit understanding that no Indian would be invited to share the privilege. And Breach Candy Swimming Club stubbornly refused to change its "Whites Only" rule.

The British government never wanted to explain its manner of ending the Raj. Perhaps, India had become a burning emblem of their shame; perhaps, India had merely become a bloody bore.

I suspect that for all his liberalism, my father secretly wished that the Raj had continued.

My father had a contentious nature that could be enflamed even by art. He seemed to like beauty. Certainly, he appreciated my godfather's sad Portuguese love songs played on a mandolin, the blues music on radio, our Oriental rugs, framed Victorian and Edwardian lithographs, and the tall, blue porcelain vase on which my mother had painted a running horse–but he sneered at the poverty of artists.

The thought of anyone starving in a garret for the sake of art provoked his ridicule. The fact that Van Gogh's paintings were now worth millions was a cruel irony of history, he liked to point out, because everybody knew how Van Gogh had starved in his lifetime. How gnarled his bony face had become, how fiercely stubby his corn-coloured short hair, how sunken his deeply pained eyes, how twisted with grime and effort his fingers. And to have to acquire notoriety by losing an ear to a prostitute–that was the penultimate monstrousness of the poor, starving artist. The ultimate horror was Van Gogh's insanity and suicide in a cornfield blighted by crows. When he saw the MGM film version of Irving Stone's *Lust For Life*, starring Kirk Douglas, one of his favourite actors, my father emphasized the agony rather than the ecstasy of the artist.

He would point to the pavement artists in Bombay who created beautiful geometric patterns and portraits in coloured chalk, and he would lament their poverty. The lament was streaked with irony, for while he did not doubt that some of these penurious artists had genuine talent, he scoffed that their only fame would come after their deaths. And what good would that be to those who were no more than scattered dust? The idea of fame through art was a fuss over very little.

I burnt with anger at such philistinism. What good was his own life, I wondered to myself. What immortality would he ever achieve? His retorts were a declaration of an underground war, a battle of instincts and impulses, to be waged without truce during my adolescence, but he seemed to relish my anger for my truculent turbulence pleased him, especially as he knew it could be easily provoked by his mockery. He was not play-acting. He was not being cheerfully aggressive. He intended his insults because, in knowing my respect for artists, he could attack the centre of my intellectual and spiritual refuge and hope for victory by humiliation.

I was to obtain my revenge in my sixteenth year.

My father wanted me to be a doctor. He attached a great deal of importance to that vocation, though his reason was based on the money, prestige, and security that doctors, especially those with a F.R.C.S. or F.R.C.P. attached to their names, seemed to enjoy. Whenever I was ill as a child, I was taken to our family doctor, old but gently wise Dr. Balchandra who always seemed to have an impressively fat medical book on his desk. Dr. Balchandra was a white Hindu in a *dhoti* and sandals, but he spoke excellent English in a soft bass voice. One of his sons was at medical school in America. Dr. Balchandra had a dispensary on the premises, and I used to watch in fascination as the pharmacist concocted powders and pills, mixtures in bright red or muddy brown and grey. But it was Dr. Balchandra I watched most intently as he slowly thumbed through his medical references or patiently examined me. Because of his age, he had a stoop, but this gave his appearance a benevolent gravity, magnified by his spectacles and carefully slow manner of speech. He was everything I imagined of a general practitioner, and what especially appealed to me was the fact that he never assumed that his vast experience could do without new technical information. He seemed to be a "readerly" doctor, who would gladly learn as he practised his vocation.

My early and sustained interest in biology, my perusal of thick medical tomes and the relish with which I sounded abstruse clinical terms ("hydrenterocele, trephining, karyoplasm, static scoliosis"), conjoined with my viewing of delicate heart surgery (through special arrangement with a young medical student), all seemed to indicate a future for me as a surgeon or specialist. In high school I took Advanced Physics and Chemistry, and enjoyed the special mark that set me and my peers apart from the general ruck of students who elected to stay within the "safe" academic confines of General Science or regular Physics-with-Chemistry.

All was well until I ventured deeper into the algebraic complexities of problem-solving in the special areas. I had always detested the formulae, equations, and theorems of mathematics, and as my classes sank into a welter of thermodynamics, valencies, refractive indices, and the laws of Boyle, Ohm, and Hooke, my enthusiasm sagged and was eventually completely deflated.

I was bright enough to transcend academic difficulties, especially those I had induced myself by a none too subtle contempt for their abstract mathematical rigour, but opting for a path of casual resistance and neglect, I blithely ignored my homework in Advanced Physics and Chemistry, keeping my mind on Shakespeare, Dickens, and Macaulay at school, and Olivier and Brando at the movies.

My ongoing warfare with my father was by now common knowledge even among certain neighbours, many of whom sided with me intellectually while urging me to show no filial disrespect. Conversation with him at the dinner table was almost non-existent, except for passing remarks on an over-cooked cutlet, a too watery stew, or a radically-spiced curry. My mother and younger sisters spoke of neighbours and social activities. I kept my silence on everything but movies, books, theatre, and fine art, unless my father passed what to me was a remark that simply screamed out for rebuttal.

I dreamed of some momentous way with which to punish him for his humiliating slights and indignities. That I was uncommonly good at drawing, painting, writing, elocution, and stage-acting seemed inordinately trivial to him. He didn't care a fig for my books; I certainly abhorred his garage grime and grease. He thought my stage and screen idols patently false; I denounced his coterie of friends for being insincere hangers-on. When I wanted quiet for study time, he'd play the radio almost at full volume, and what was worse, permit my sister Elma to indulge her sickening infatuation with rock-'n'-roll music.

"Well, I can't study with all this noise!" I'd protest.

There would be a brief lowering of the volume, but eventually Elma would connive to reset the bass and treble dials to her liking and then would gloat openly at yet another victory under my father's aegis.

I did not rant, though venom curdled within me. Of course, I did not mention my lack of progress in those subjects most important to a medical career.

Today, the old feud and my father's slights are overshadowed by years that have catharted all the rottenness. But then, when I was sixteen, my malignant intent was probably a sign of willed corruption.

My teachers, peers, and family expected that I would obtain a First in my Cambridge G.C.E.'s, and, indeed, I had enough Distinctions and High Credits in English Language, Literature, French, History, and Art to warrant such expectation. However, Mathematics, Physics, and Chemistry–that deadly trio–loomed like a sullen cloud in a bright heaven. I, of course, neglected them with a cold heart. No one could say that I had chosen to do so against my will or that I had not understood the consequences of my choice. I dreamed of getting even with my father, though even then I did not clearly envisage what shape his pain and disintegration would take. I would make an effort in those subjects I liked and would allow myself to fail whatever he most wanted me to conquer.

I think I even dreamed of possible scenarios: how I'd laugh inwardly at his shock at my catastrophic results in Science and Math, how he'd have his proud hope dashed without any recompense, how I'd rub his wound with a stingingly offhand comment, how he'd have to confess his brutish mistakes in our troubled relationship.

But I also knew the consequences to my own pride. I would be considered a palpable disappointment by my school. Even there, teachers tended to value the sciences higher than the arts. Moreover, failure in Science would probably cost me a First.

While I yearned for a grand, perverse gesture, I knew that its context would never be light and free for me.

When my final results arrived, with the inevitable failures in Physics and Chemistry and a bare pass in Mathematics, I blushed. I did think that my general average would sneak me into a First Class, but I had now defeated myself as well as my father.

The academic embarrassment did not last long. I distinguished myself as an university undergraduate, and I laboured hard in a literary vineyard. I did become a doctor, a Ph.D., that is, and so my father could, if he had wanted, have referred to me as "Doctor." He never did.

Was what I had done really revenge? Was it, rather, a rather wrong-headed attempt to deny him the pride in a dutiful son? Was it a scheme to force him to declare his own wounding, his own vulnerability? His pride was subject to my will to define myself on my own terms.

Even when I was a teenager, he tried to make me responsible for his future. Because we quarrelled frequently–it was constitutional, virtually genetically decreed–he always tried to cast me as an ingrate, the eldest-born who would remain indifferent to his needs in old age.

"Elma will look after me," he maintained self-assuredly.

Anger prompted me to shoot back: "Good!"

Having successfully provoked me, he settled back in smug satisfaction.

Was it such early confrontations that conditioned me into keeping my distance from him when, indeed, he had become dependent on the visitations and consolations of his children?

He kept most of his brusque affection for Elma or my mother. I was mostly relieved.

And so the silence between us grew wider and deeper.

Then he was eventually old, though he did not go gently into the harvesting darkness. Even into his early eighties, he did not identify with senior citizens, refusing to join the social club in his condominium apartment. "Ach, they're old fogies!" he would complain. This was when he himself had found his eyes growing milkier, his always defective hearing becoming increasingly deficient, and his feet turning to stone.

The truth was that he couldn't make small talk, couldn't discourse on subjects that were not immediately within his small circle of interest.

"She's old!" he would say dismissively of an acquaintance, or "He's getting on!"–which were his way of detaching himself from the "inescapable lousiness" of growing old. Yet he himself was gradually becoming restless by the fact of his own futility.

Making a litany of complaints about his own aches and pains–in his neck, shoulder, elbows, feet–he would telephone my sister, Audrey, and her husband, Peter, at least six times a day, requesting cigarettes or more Scotch or something that was barely on the rim of necessity. He expected immediate gratification, but his real need was for company. All he had in his apartment, growing increasingly smokier and greyer with nicotine, was the futility of objects that would clearly outlast him. Bottles of after-shave lotion, containers of talcum powder, an electric shaver, an electric kettle, a barely used toaster, a wrought-iron glass-top breakfast table, chipped and scratched, with wrought-iron chairs lacquered a lime green, a portable radio that blared into his ears, and a ticking clock set on the dining-table and which he frequently consulted in a banal ritual of measuring time that was slowly ebbing from his life. Unable to see clearly without the aid of a magnifying glass, he would hold the clock close to his face to read the oversize numbers.

"What day is it?" he would ask five or six times in the course of one of my visits.

Lost in his loneliness, he surely could take no instruction from time. The almost ceaseless repetition of the query, "What day is it?" enflamed my irritation. Conversation, real conversation with an exchange of directed energies and purposeful rhetoric, was impossible. He still refused to hear what I said, unless it conformed to what he wanted to hear. Sometimes it seemed that he insisted on hearing the opposite of what I told him, perversely repeating to himself his own twisted version of what he had deliberately misheard.

"There's nothing wrong with his hearing," my mother used to say. "He hears perfectly well when he wants to." She would indicate his ability to eavesdrop on her conversation while he was in an adjoining room, presumably out of earshot.

But that was in another time, before his body did in fact begin to deteriorate visibly.

Our history of conflict had been marked by reciprocal refusals of each other's needs, desires, and expectations. He had wanted me to be a surgeon; I had selected teaching and the arts. He had expected palpable gratitude for his role as a father; I had wanted a different sort of father.

Both of us had squandered our life together, and now apart from each other, except for my monthly visits or family reunions on special occasions, we were continuing to feel the knife edge at each other's back.

No wonder the only sounds in his apartment were those of the amplified radio and the ticking clock. Those sounds beat against the smoke-stained walls, infiltrated the furniture and carpet, and soaked into my father's ears. They did not stop him from talking to himself, and they couldn't shrivel his need to commune with the ghosts of his mother, wife, or daughter.

I can only imagine what he uttered to himself. His depressions, complaints, dilemmas. Perhaps a sudden truth in the middle of a fragmented thought. But no narrative, except that tortuous one of his first history, shrunk with the labour of remembering, his energy depleted by the task of surviving life and reconstructing posthumous facts, influential events, political circumstances.

Despite this eerie disintegration of his everyday life, he was not prepared to die. His will was always stronger than his body, though he maintained the body by his perpetual hunger.

What he probably liked best about my visits was the food I took him from Indian restaurants in Malton. He, who had had no especial liking for samosas, *biryani*, or spicy rich curries when he was in India, now relished each bite, each swallow.

I would serve us both a portion on plates and wrap up the rest to refrigerate. Then we would eat together, in silence, and I watched as he savoured the food with an extravagant pleasure. We had strangely grown intimate by this shared meal.

I was transfixed by his face. He seemed to concentrate on every bite, chew, and swallow, and his dim eyes glowed with satisfaction. Every pastry flake, potato sliver, or chicken scrap was a pearl in his mouth. But it was difficult not to see a shadow behind this lust: the shadow of that wild hunger of his boyhood, when he had cried with abandonment.

My sympathy was an invisible current. If he sensed it, he did not say. I let it remain invisible, forsaking explicit declaration in the further silence.

There is no outcome in this weaving, this casual wandering, with joy, suffering, death, transformation, arrivals and departures, surface tensions, curvatures, all flickering in the same company, a welter from which one chaos is displaced, perhaps, into another, and something born out of this flux.

If this were fiction, it would move toward resolution. Problems and complications would be defined, understood, pushed toward closure. But this is memoir: it has moved backward to the mystery of origins. It has sought traces, gestures, patterns in my parents' lives in order to fashion from these a connection between their lives and mine. It has sought to shore up fragments into a whole.

Function is surmise, all linked to our births–fragmentary associations, interruptions, a respiration, a sense of loss under the slow or quick movements. Nevertheless, I glide on ink and paper, a nomad and resident alien, imagining mortality, its unrest and intricacies, imagining evolving love, thousands of celebratory words folded into my interrupted grief and pain.

I compose this in my white study, newly carpetted, well-lined with books, thousands of word-artists with their numinous brushstrokes on paper, minds moving into my silence, sensations of myth weaving well the perpetuation of lives, of imagination, of memory speaking back, of remembering tomorrows.

I have little that belonged to him, barely any knowledge of his first history beyond what he told us and what I have been able to confirm by my reading. All the photographs of him are from the time of his marriage, and there is no letter, no missive in his own hand, not even after his marriage–except for greeting cards and his last will and testament, sealed with a virtually indecipherable signature.

So everything of his traumatized heart I can only imagine, having recorded some of it almost near the end of his life, and only surmising the invisible, the shadows he had confronted.

What survives of him in physical things are discrete objects: the intricately hand-carved walnut-wood lampstand given to him upon his retirement from French Motors; patent leather shoes he hardly wore because his feet swelled too grotesquely owing to poor circulation; a cloth cap that had made him seem too indiscriminately working-class as he walked to the shopping centre; drably conservative ties and suits stubbornly old-fashioned.

I was my mother's son more than his–intellectually, psychologically, morally–but I am reminded by family and acquaintances that I resemble much of him in some of my moods and tones. I have his genes; I therefore have his imprint. And though most of my life has been a conscious battle against his image, I can no longer define myself wholly *against* his example. I can no longer be insolent to my fate.

Clark Blaise has written: "We are born to strangers we must learn to love, in a town or country we would not have chosen, into a tribe that defines and restricts our growth. We spend a lifetime overcoming the givens, only to turn from the distant vantage point of fifty years when the parents are gone, to look back and say: this is what I am, something no larger, no freer than they made me."

Had he merely wanted all of us to become with him a community of pain, to share a lifetime of unspeakable emotion?

We, who have never suffered as much and know only the names for such pain, tolerate images as livid as wounds. We may spend our days writing of the dead and then find consolation at night in quiescent sleep.

He, however, never learned to write of poised or wrenched life. He had seen too much in his first history lesson, his tortured boyhood, to know what to select and articulate in the next.

We did not know how to share his pain, how to make it as intimate as love.

It was only at moments of family loss–my sister's, my mother's unnecessary deaths–that my father and I entered an area of greater tenderness. Then we addressed each other with unabashed truth, our mouths cleansing themselves with memories. But these were brief respites from trivial gestures remembered almost endlessly or large phantoms of incomplete lives.

When he died, alone, possibly in the middle of uttering a name, it was one more moment from a life that I missed.

All I saw at the end was his old face with its mouth gaping wide. Ceaselessly hungry for life, for breath with which to utter his curses against enemies. Now a dark open circle that had swallowed his history, but unable, it seemed, to utter the password for a peaceful eternity. O!...Nothing! Denied dignity and grace yet again.

We had both been diminished by the other when we could have been enlarged.

I leaned to touch and kiss his forehead, remembering how wrinkled and feeble his hands had been the last time I had held them while he was slowly sinking away.

Grief was somehow mixed with relief. He and I would no longer be pulsing contraries, each stubborn with a faith in different infinities. He and his murdered tribe were now ever-receding soundwaves in our uncertain galaxy, whereas I was left to find a voice for his history and my future.

To speak of my grief and relief without mentioning pain would be a half-truth. Grief and pain arose out of my remoteness from my father. I could feel his pain, I considered his life important for what it achieved from the unspeakable void, and I extended to him at least the bare consideration of a dutiful son, if not the warm tenderness and patient support he so clearly desired. Our relationship changed over the years; he grew a little softer toward me, but this came too late to make me feel more empathetic. The silences between us never shrank. Perhaps he was afraid that his remarks or complaints would be overwhelmed by my arrogant, impatient retorts.

I still wonder if he ever knew the psychic deprivation I felt with him. I know that some of this feeling came to me despite his good will.

"Your father can't help it." I heard that numerous times from family members and family friends. His history had been an aching wound, and I had always wanted to look into this wound more closely, though I felt, as his years fell into the yellow leaf, uneasy about drawing closer to him. His dark side, his wildness had been overwhelming. I couldn't forget his verbal abuse, his public shaming of us by his erratic behaviour when he was drunk, his roughness to my mother, his rages and paranoia. I had not forgiven him for making me afraid of him.

Age and experience, however, have taught me that our fathers alone don't fully give us their wounds.

"Father and son in the East! Their relationship can scarcely be compared with the superficial contact of European parents and children. Whoso sees his father sees God. For that father is the last link in a long, unbroken chain of ancestors, binding all men to Adam, and hence to the origin of creation. And yet whoso sees his son sees God. For his son is the next link, binding humans to the Last Judgment, the end of all things, the consummation. Must not so holy a relationship be timid and sparing of words?" (Franz Werfel, *The Forty Days of Musa Dagh*.)

My father's chain of ancestors was split, though by his very name alone he remained linked to the first Adam. As for me, I am a writer who seeks a consummation without finally judging him.

He died without ever telling me if he had retained any faith in man, but I know instinctively that he willed for me a survival against despair. He never said aloud whether he thought a writer disappeared so much into imagination as to be absent from the real world, but I know in my bones that he wished for me to find a place in whatever world where I could bear witness to a devastation of grace.

"Now the gold which belongs to Horus comes to your fingernails and makes you immortal." Ancient Egyptian wisdom which amounts to the companionship of ancestors and, more than this, a blessing.

Perhaps this meditative journey which has me stirring waters of memory is really my father's final will, and all the thoughts and feelings, the wild ecstasies and tender transports, the nostalgic reminiscences and imaginative projections are responses to his invisible beckoning.

He died with his mouth a gaping wound, and if I could now touch his lips with some of these words, I feel that my fingertips would turn to gold.

When I am in a poetic mood, I think of the unicorn as an Armenian creature because legend has it that it was the only animal that would not enter Noah's ark. It stayed outside and swam.

No one knows if it survived or drowned.

Many Armenians of the older generations have a saying: "When the past is behind you, keep it there."

But this is a gesture of defeat in an age that promotes denial. This way the intrusive past cannot be channelled; this way Isaiah can be silenced in the void from where he would cry, "Truly Thou art a God Who hides Himself."

Those few Armenians who survived the slaughter and are still alive often start their memories with the phrase, *Djamangeen gar oo chagar*. A long time ago, there was and there wasn't.

This way the past can be invoked in snatches, our human insecurity and doubt comforted by the fact that lyric memory can partially fill the void.

The old Armenians say: "*Kna merir yegooz sirem*. Die, come back, I love you." It is death that makes us wise, while mortification teaches us to love and become new.

These old Armenians also have a special sense of the word "soul." They often invoke the word *hokee* in various modes: *Hokeet dal*: to have soul energy. *Hokeet seerem*: I love your soul. *Sourp hokee*: holy spirit. *Hokee kaloust*: coming of the spirit.

I now say to my dead father: You were a father and you were not, in a time that was and a time that was not. *Hokeet seerem*. I love your soul, your fighter's soul. Paradoxically, I love the fierceness that had frightened me as a child.

"Our blood is a strange poem."

– Lorne Shirinian

I loved my father, despite his glaring faults, but it was a strange love: part filial duty; part blood-driven instinct. I wish that my love could have been expressed in ways beyond my grudging visits and dutiful gifts to him. Even as I wept when composing my eulogy for his funeral, I wondered whether I should hate myself for writing about him when I had tried on numerous occasions to refuse him as a father.

"I have always hated myself for that
and do so even now
for having written about it
We lose our parents
and attempt redemption through poems & stories
our savage testament scripted
all that is left to us now
orphan offspring of orphans"

– Lorne Shirinian,
History of Armenia and Other Fictions

I once wrote an Armenian elegy in English. I dedicated it to Michael Arlen because of his poignant memoir, *Passage to Ararat*, which had inspired it. But I have never met Michael Arlen, and he does not know me or my writing.

The poem was really about my father and me.

Memory is a soft thudding of clubs.
At a monument for martyrs:
a chauvinism about suffering,
a deep thing for deep-sea souls
twisting and turning.
History is a colophon:
shipwrecked words stuffed in bottles
drifting get help soon
to no one.
But survival's a world's edge bargain
a truce for dreaming more modestly.
Survival's, too, the circle
in which the young
will set their fathers free.